Endorsement

Time and time again, it has been emphasized that the achievement of success is not something that will come to anyone easily. Success entails a lot of passion, dedication and discipline in order to be achieved by anyone. Only with great sacrifices can a person be deserving of achieving success.

If you are serious about success in your life, *The Art of Success* is a must read. Pastor Geoffrey Kilonzo has explored areas of concern as far as succeeding in this life is concerned: Learning from failures, setting goals, the power of knowledge and information, creativity, positiveness, rising above fear, makers of destiny, diligence and enthusiasm, giving, investment, professional pride, God's fear and honoring spiritual fathers.

God's wish and prayer is that we succeed in all areas in this life. He desires that we live comfortably and in plenty. 3 John1:2 states, "Beloved, I pray that in all respects you may prosper and be in good health, just as your soul prospers."

The Art of Success has the tips and guides you need to make your life one big success story. It provides you with step by step instructions to start you on the road to happiness, prosperity, health and success. Success in everything you do can really be yours! Life can be anything you make it, and success, riches and rewards are just waiting for you. Discover the *The Art of Success* and finally start living your dreams.

After reading the this book, you will gain insight into all the things you have been doing right all along. Even more important, you will be able to identify the mistakes that have derailed you, and use that knowledge to your advantage from now on. It's never what you *are,* but what you *do.*

Pastor Geoffrey Kilonzo the Author of this book; 'THE ART OF SUCCESS', is a pastor of Redeemed Gospel Church in Nairobi. He is one of the upcoming sons in the ministry whom we have high hopes in to bring a shift to this generation and a positive impact to young people.

Pastor Geoffrey is also a contributor to the Endtime Magazine, a publication of Redeemed Gospel Church. He has influenced many young Christian professionals and businesspeople in and outside Kenya through his entrepreneurial skills, speaking talent and art of writing. Having risen from a slum dweller in Mathare to a vessel of honour, he is a living testimony by himself of how God can change your life. This book is applicable to all levels of people from slum dwellers who want to succeed, to successful people who want to maintain their successful life.

I am sure this book and his ministry will inspire you to rise to greater heights.

-Bishop Dr. Arthur Kitonga; Founder and Apostolic Bishop of Redeemed Gospel Churches

This book "THE ART OF SUCCESS" is very well written, edited and published. It's a work of excellence. It is a mine of information. Glory to God for the great heights He is taking you to.

- Apostle Catherine Kagiri, M.A. Housing Administration and Senior Pastor of Worship and Restoration Ministries (WARM)

I met Geoffrey when he was organizing the Kenya Diaspora London Expo. My company was interested in participating as we were launching a product relevant to that clientele. His passion, commitment, and determination to make the Expo successful was outstanding, to say the least. He took personal responsibility for each and every phase of the project, and as his client, that made me have the peace of mind I needed to trust him and his grand plan. Needless to say, he saw the Expo through to its most successful finish. We then became great acquaintances and I even agreed to mentor him through life's interesting turns. I was truly humbled that he asked me to write this foreword.

Funny thing is, when I asked people how they define their personal success and how they would know if it had arrived...very few of them could. The ones who did defined success as having loads of cash and/or fame. This book, then, is critical in helping a majority of us to actually put pen to paper and define what you want to achieve; the journey there is made easier by Geoffrey. Once you know where you are going he equips you with the necessary tools to get you there successfully. The tools Geoffrey has given us are simple, realistic, and applicable across the board.

What I love most about this book is that it compiles all the learning and theories of great writers like Stephen Covey, John Mason, Zig Ziglar, Wallace D. Wattles, and John Maxwell, not forgetting, most of all, our Holy Bible. He has extracted a winning array of extremely useful data and quotes to help us replicate the habits of successful people and their successes as well.

To encourage us to have that most important internal dialogue that questions our every move so that we know what we are doing right and most importantly how to overcome those mental barriers to our success.

To me, it all starts with personal discipline, sacrifice, perseverance, and the hunger to learn new things, and unlearn some old things too. Success is an all-rounded habit, a constant physical, academic, spiritual, and mental craving to get the best in everything you do...the rewards will soon follow. It comes from within, starting with your mind and heart; from knowing how to set goals and track your performance; from celebrating success despite how small the success; from learning from mistakes, but most of all from a positive attitude! Thank you Mr. Kilonzo for putting all this into perspective!

- **Karen Rimita-Mwanza,**
Senior Banker and a Financial consultant.

THE ART OF SUCCESS

GEOFFREY N. KILONZO

WESTBOW
PRESS®
A DIVISION OF THOMAS NELSON
& ZONDERVAN

eaglewingsconsultants@gmail.com
+254 725 328 386

Cover design by Andrew Longilai

WestBow Press books may be ordered through booksellers or by contacting:

WestBow Press
A Division of Thomas Nelson & Zondervan
1663 Liberty Drive
Bloomington, IN 47403
www.westbowpress.com
1 (866) 928-1240

ISBN: 978-1-5127-1609-2 (sc)

Library of Congress Control Number: 2015916940

Print information available on the last page.

WestBow Press rev. date: 10/26/2015

Contents

Endorsement i
Dedication ix
Appreciation xi
Introduction xiii

Chapter 1   Learn From Failures 1
Chapter 2   Setting Goals 7
Chapter 3   Acquire Knowledge & Information 28
Chapter 4   Be Creative 51
Chapter 5   Be Positive 64
Chapter 6   Rise Above Fear 77
Chapter 7   Embrace Makers of Destiny 89
Chapter 8   Be Diligent & Enthusiastic 96
Chapter 9   Practice Giving 109
Chapter 10 Learn to Invest 129
Chapter 11 Have Professional Pride 136
Chapter 12 Have the Fear of God 143
Chapter 13 Honour Your Spiritual Fathers 149

Bibliography 187
Other Readings 189

Dedication

This book is dedicated to all people in business, school, employed, or in Church ministry, for them to succeed in their endeavors. I also dedicate it to my beloved wife, Liz, my awesome son, Destiny Amani and my lovely daughter Angel Fanaka. Your patience, prayers, and encouragement made it easy for me to achieve this goal.

Appreciation

First, I thank the Almighty God for inspiring me to write this book. The ability to read and write comes from the Lord.

Special thanks to my darling wife Elizabeth for the moral support and encouragement. You sacrificed a lot and you were patient with me during the long nights I spent reading and writing. My dear wife Liz, My beloved children; Destiny and Angel I love you with all the passion.

Many thanks also to my spiritual father, Reverend Chris, you spent a lot of time mentoring me in ministry. Your correction, encouragement, prayers, and love have made me a true servant. Your labor was not in vain.

I wish to thank Reverend Josephine Kitonga (a mother of a great family; Redeemed Gospel Churches Inc) for your contribution through your continued teachings on leadership. You changed many lives Mum including mine and may your reward in heaven be great even as the Lord tells you *"Well Done Thou Good and Faithful Servant!"*

Special thanks to Linda Okero for the work of proof reading. George Mbira for believing in me and for your mentorship. Firm friends group, Virgin properties company partners; Carol and team, Big Worship team, LAMP prayer team and the entire Rafiki Microfinance Bank team. Thanks for your support.

To my friends, mentors and close co-workers in the ministry; Rev Peter Mwangangi (A true spiritual covering in my life), Rev John B. Kitonga a true inspiration to me, amongst others.

Many thanks to my dad and mum (David and Jestina Kilonzo), my brother Jose, and my two sisters Ruth and Mary; I love you all.

Many thanks also to the members of Redeemed Gospel Church, Sportsview- Kasarani. I couldn't find a warmer and supportive family like this. You have always received me as your beloved pastor and given me the moral support I needed. To everyone else who supported me I say GOD BLESS YOU ALL.

Introduction

Being successful is an inalienable right of every human being. Our being born on the earth is not an accident, but it is a deliberate effort to plan and position us on the earth for certain purposes. God does not intend to make some of His creations successful and others failures. It is we who choose our path, whether consciously or unconsciously, towards success or failure. Success is not a certain end but a journey to the desired end.

Success gives meaning and purpose to the journey of life. Success is not and never has been about getting or achieving anything. True success is about what you must be in order to attract everything you require to live the life you have always dreamed of living.

Success depends on mastering the art of success. This art transforms a hard-working person to a smart-working person. It transforms a failure to a successful person. Through the art of success, you can be sure to blossom where you are planted.

By definition, art is *the principles or methods governing any craft or branch of learning or the skill in conducting any human activity.* Thus, you put into place the principles of success and develop your skills by doing what successful people do; soon you too will be among those who have succeeded in life.

You can become successful in whatever you do. By following these principles, you don't have to change your job, business, marriage, church, or what you are doing in order to be successful. Try applying the nuggets of wisdom given in this book into whatever you are doing and watch out for the result.

The successful people you admire and desire to be like have a way that they do their things. There are certain principles or methods which govern the process of success, and once these methods are learned and obeyed by anyone, that person will become successful.

It is the same with the art of success; if you do not follow these methods you remain a failure.

You may be the biggest failure ever and be deeply in debt. You may have no friends, influence, or resources. But if you begin to follow these principles, you will infallibly begin to move forward, for like causes must produce like effects. The art of success is a craft that will transform you positively.

If you can duplicate the habits of successful people, you will be able to duplicate their results as well. It is not a certain location, or a certain type of business or a certain career that makes people successful. It is doing things that successful people do that will make you successful.

Chapter One

Learn From Failures

When you fail, learn the lessons and forget the details

Learn From Failures

I t is not how many times you fall that counts, but the one time you do it right. We all experience failure and make mistakes. Failure does not mean that nothing has been accomplished. Successful people have many counts of failures. Those who expect nothing in life are never disappointed. People who have no failures have no victories either. If you never try anything, you will never fail at any given time. When you try and fail, learn the lessons and forget the details.

Do not fear to fail for it is better to fail trying something than to succeed in doing nothing. Success is defined by getting it right once, and not by how many times you failed.

When you fail, learn the lessons and forget the details. The devil likes reminding you of the details of your failures but learn how to ignore the details.

Build on the lessons of your failures and when you fall, pick up something. In every failure there is a lesson that God is teaching you. You rise up better and wiser. Learn to fall and roll, like a soccer player. When you fall don't rise from where you have fallen; roll and rise up at another level.

Understand that you can't travel the road of success without a puncture. Failure is a teacher who teaches us how to approach life differently. When you fall look at what you have left and not what you have lost. Do not give up the fight because you have failed. You can't tell how close you are to success; it may be near when it seems far so stick to the fight even when you are hardest hit. It's when things seem worst that you must not quit.

> *We are pressed on every side by troubles, but not bruised, and broken. We are perplexed because we don't know why things happen as they do, but we don't give up and quit. We are hunted down, but God never abandon us, we get knocked down but we get up again and keep going.*
> **2 Corinthians 4:8-9** (Living Bible)

We all fail and make mistakes, but we don't get finished in our failure; we can rise up again and move on. We should always make our failures the bridges that we use to cross to success and not see them as barricades.

Paul knew that being a Christian does not exclude you from facing the world's challenges. Rather it equips you to live positively and victoriously in the midst of it all. He indicated that in our problems God is always working on us and walking with us.

Failures provide an opportunity to grow not to die. When you face the music today, someday you will lead the band. Every time we face a failure we learn a lesson that makes us become masters of that which made us fail. We are like a tea bag; we can never taste until we are put in hot water.

Everybody has a midnight hour, a time when you wish you never existed. Friends desert you and it turns completely dark. If you are in that situation, remember: it's always darkest when it is near dawn. Your morning is almost come.

Weeping may endure for a night but joy comes in the morning
Psalm 30:5

If you fail do not stay down for it is not how far you fall but how high you bounce back that makes the difference. No one ever achieved a worthwhile success and did not at one time or another fail. If you have tried to do something and failed you are better off than if you had tried to do nothing and succeeded. If you are not making mistakes, you are not risking enough.

You must get up from your failures and go on. The best way to go on after a failure is to learn the lesson and forget the details. Failure can become a weight to weigh you down but it can also give you wings to fly higher. Understand that falling in water does not make one drawn but staying in the water.

Something interesting about failure is that, in the multitude of it some people grow wings while others buy crutches. Choose your portion today.

Someone said that success is failure turned inside out. You can never tell how close you are to victory; it may be near when it seems far. So stick to the fight when you are hardest hit, it's when things seem worst that you must not quit.

Falling is part of life but we have a God who will not allow us to be cast down. Every time we fall He upholds us with His hand.

You are not the first one to face failures; the greatest and most successful business people failed many times before becoming what they are.

Theodore Roosevelt said it is better to dare mighty things, to win glorious triumphs, even though checked by failure than to rank with those poor spirits who neither enjoy much nor suffer much because they live in the gray twilight that knows not victory or defeat.

The riskiest thing you can do in life is to take too many precautions and never have any failures or mistakes. The death of your dream will not be brought about by trying to fail but by failing to try. Keep trying; your victory is a few trials ahead. People will never remember you by the number of times you failed but by the achievements you made after failing.

Do not dwell on your past, forget it and forge foreword. You can't walk backward into the future. The past should be a spring board to your future. Don't let your past mistakes become memorials. You may stay too far in the past that the future goes before you get there.

Apostle Paul says in **Philippians 3:13-14** - *Forgetting what is behind and straining toward what is ahead, I press on toward the goal to win the prize for which God has called me heavenward in Christ Jesus*
And in Colossians 3:2a *set your minds on things above...*

Get out of your past and follow your dream. God is waiting for your there not here. Get ready to go there. 'There' is in the future not in the past or in the present.

When you look back at your life, you will regret the things you didn't do more than the things you did. Your future contains more happiness than any past you can remember. Our God is a God of tomorrow and not yesterday. You will become so miserable trying to walk with a tomorrow God in the past.

Nevertheless you must avoid more failures in the future. This can be possible by avoiding possible causes of failures. The challenges and problems we face daily cannot be solved at the same level we were when we created them. As we look around us and within us and recognize the problems we create as we live and interact within others, we begin to realize that these are deep fundamental problems that cannot be solved on the superficial level on which they were created. Our failures need a higher level of thinking and action to overcome.

We must learn to take responsibility for our failures and not blame anybody for them. The solutions of our lives are better solved using the inside-out approach to life.

When you fail, look inside you for a solution. Many people do the opposite, Outside-In. They blame others for their failures.

No man has a chance to enjoy permanent success until he begins to look inside for the real cause of all his mistakes.

Chapter Two

Setting Goals

Life is a goldmine

Set Goals

A goal is an atom of what it is before it is. Goal setting is an act of faith. It is faith that calls things that are not as though they are. It pleases God when we set goals for it is without faith that we cannot please Him. But with faith we can (see Hebrews 11:6).

No matter what goals we are working toward in life, we must have a strong desire to achieve them. If your goals aren't important to you then you've got nothing to lose by quitting. You probably won't summon enough motivation to get it done. Think about the last time you set a goal, like starting a new business, beginning a church fellowship, going for higher education, etc. If you were not absolutely 100% committed when you got started you likely wouldn't have stayed long with it. You would have been fired up at the beginning, like most people are when they set a goal, but as time went on you would either encounter obstacles that slow your momentum, or you would just lose the passion and fire for the end result. Hence you would quit.

Making positive changes in your life is no different. No matter how hard you work at the beginning, if the changes you're trying to make are not crucially important to you, you just won't have the determination to see them all the way through.

Before you begin working on any goal, first ask yourself how important the end result is to you. How badly do you want it? How hard are you willing to work for it? What will happen if you don't make it? Will you be able to accept the consequences, or are they simply unthinkable? Be honest with yourself. Your answers to these questions will determine your probability of success.

There is no achievement without goals, said Robert J. McKain. Goal setting is the most powerful tool you need to achieve success. Goals keep you focused, motivated, and give you a step-by-step plan to success. If you set no goals you can't achieve any measure of success. Life has a meaning when goals are established, and true success is achieved only when we set high goals.

Goals have a deadline (expiry date), goals are specific, goals are put in writing, and goals have a clear step-by-step plan. You should begin setting high goals and start working towards them. Stop dreaming and get into action.

George Washington Carver, an African-American scientist who lived during the civil war, was the man who single-handedly changed lives of South American farmers in that era. Early in his career, Carver urged farmers to plant peanuts when the first crop came in. However, there was no market and having every sense of failure in him, he retreated to his lab to pray. Caver could not face his students and friends at this time.

He committed himself to prayer for misleading the people. He begged for forgiveness from his Savior.

After prayer and setting the goal of finding as many uses of peanuts as quickly as he could, George discovered over 300 uses of peanuts. He discovered among them peanut butter, peanut oil, paper, paint, and paste from peanut. In a short time, peanut farmers could barely meet the public demand for the crop.

It is important to be specific while setting your goals. Know what you want. There is a great power in goal-setting. The Bible in Proverbs 11:27 says -

He who seeks good finds good will, but evil comes to him who searches for it.

The Power Within

Set high goals and God will enable you to achieve them. *Now to him who is able to do exceedingly, abundantly above all that we ask or think, according to the power that worketh in us.* **Ephesians 3:20** (King James Version)

You don't achieve your goals through your might or your power. God told Zechariah in **4:6** (King James Version) -

It is neither by might nor by power, but my spirit, saith the Lord of hosts.

There is a power that works in our lives from within. God has put the potential in you to succeed. This is the power that creates wealth, overcomes challenges, guides us, and reveals secrets to us.

Deuteronomy 8:18 (New Living Translation) *He is the one who gives you power to be successful, in order to fulfill the covenant he confirmed to your ancestors with an oath.*

What is this power within? The Bible says in **Acts 1:8** –
*And you shall receive power (Dunamis) when the Holy Spirit comes
on you...*

Dunamis is a Greek word meaning act of power in
Young's dictionary; miraculous power, ability in Strong's
dictionary; natural capability, inherent power; capability
of anything, ability to perform anything; then, absolutely,
not merely power capable of action, but, power in action
in Bullinger's dictionary. In summary it means; **ability,
efficiency and might**.

This statement was given by Jesus answering a question
by the disciples about times. And Jesus began by saying in
Acts 1:7

*"It is not for you to know the times or seasons which the
father hath put in his own power"*

In other words what you are asking for or whatever you
want, is in the power that am about to give you. It is written
in **John 1:12** (King James Version)

As many as received him, to them gave he power to become....
It finishes with *... sons.*

Where the word sons appears you can put whatever you
want to become. Do you want to become successful, in business
or career? There is a power to become. This is the power that
works in us. Christ in us is the power that works in us.

There is promise that God gave to make you successful and wealthy. All you need is to set goals and go for them. God is taking the responsibility to make you successful. Paul achieved success in ministry by understanding the art of goal-setting. He said 1 Corinthians 9:26

> *Therefore I do not run like a man running aimlessly,* (without goals), *I do not fight like a man beating the air.*

Like Paul, you must have goals that you live for, otherwise your life will be aimless and therefore without purpose.

When you are setting goals remember you were not created to be everything. You are best in one thing and that is what you should seek to discover. Follow your passion even when it seems to be the most difficult job.

To set high goals in life you need a strong conviction and passion. A poor man is not only the one without money but one without passion too.

Goals make more meaning when they are set towards the direction of your destiny. Using the shape principle, it is easy to discover your destiny then follow it with passion.

Follow your 'shape'. This can help you discover who you are.

Job 10:8 states
'Your hands shaped me and made me'.

Isaiah 43:21
'The people I have shaped for myself will broadcast my praises'.

Shape stands for:

S - Spiritual gifts

These are special empowered abilities for serving God that are given to believers. Your spiritual gifts reveal one way of discovering who you are in life.

H - Heart

Listening to your heart is a very important key to realizing your purpose in life. Your heart represents the source of all your motivation i.e. what you love to do and what you care about most. Your heart reveals the real you. Listen to your heart.

> *As waters reflect a face, so a man's heart reflects a man*
> **Proverbs 27:19**

A - Abilities

These are the natural talents you were born with. Some have natural abilities in talking, athletics, singing, etc. God honors natural abilities and He empowers them to give you a destiny. Nurture those natural talents you were born with.

When God wanted Moses to build the tabernacle, He directed him to a man who earned his living and had succeeded through his natural abilities.

> Exodus 31:3-4
> *The Lord said to Moses, "I have chosen Bezalel son of Uri....*
> *and I have filled him with the spirit of God with skill, ability*
> *and knowledge in all kinds of crafts to make artistic design..."*

The natural abilities you have are strong indicators of what God wants you to become.

P - Personality

We should use our personality to understand what we were made to be in order to rise above failure in life. We are all unique in our DNA. Some personalities are introverts while others are extroverts. Some people love routine others love variety, some are thinkers others are feelers, some are sanguine others choleric, and yet others melancholic. Knowing your personality is a step towards discovering your purpose in life. Your personality will affect how, where, and in what you can succeed in life. You can never do what I do the way I do it, because you do it in a manner consistent with the personality God gave you to experience fullest satisfaction and fruitfulness.

E - Experience

Experience contributes a lot in revealing to us where we belong. This may be from family experience, what you learnt either from your mother, father, or relative, to educational experience on which was your favorite subject in school, to vocational experience. What jobs have you been most effective in and enjoyed most even if it was not your choice career?

In my working experience I have learnt that nothing just happens, rather all things work out as God's plan to push us to our destiny of success.

From one job to another, God took me through different experiences. Some jobs were good others were stressful. I didn't seem able to reach a comfort zone. However before one door closed, another door opened for me.

In the process I came to realize that one job led to the other, and that the former was always a training ground for the latter. Mostly, one, some, or all of these experiences will serve as a preparation for what you will become in life. You become a master of what you have experienced more than of what you have been taught in class. God allows you to go through painful experiences to equip you to fulfill your divine purpose in life.

The brief above can help those who have not known their purpose to discover who they are today. Setting goals must be towards the direction you are going in life. Don't just follow the easy way while you don't belong there. The path of least resistance only made rivers like men, crooked.

God has placed within each one of us the potential and opportunity of succeeding.

Ecclesiastes 9:11
For time and chance happen to them all

Take responsibility for your life and set goals towards your success. At least have something to do. Life's heaviest burden is to have nothing to carry. If you fail to plan you plan to fail.

Below are basic steps of setting **G.O.A.L.S;**

G - Gather information

O - Organize yourself and your steps (first things first)

A - Act now

L - Look back and see if you are still on track

S - Set new goals always.

I. G- Gather information

The act of gathering information about your plan is like a foundation; the deeper the foundation the stronger the building. The more the information you have the stronger the idea. When storms come the idea will not be broken down but it shall stand the test of time.

Never begin anything without researching. Thorough gathering of information helps to understand the approach you will give your idea and also the pitfalls to avoid.

Moses sent the twelve spies to go and explore the land of Canaan so that they can know how to attack the city (see Numbers 13).

You must do a good research before you start acting. Do you know what you want to do? Do you know your objectives? Do you know the end result?

Learn to cross the bridge before you get there. You should be aware of the mountains and valleys on your way. It is better to spend time prospecting and planning than to act blindly. When you spend time prospecting and planning you will not waste time when you launch.

Get advice from people who have succeeded in what you are planning to do. When you don't get advice, your plans fail. But with advice you are sure of victory in your plans. The wise man said in Proverbs 11:14 –

For lack of guidance a nation falls. But many advisers make victory sure

II. O- Organize yourself and your steps

To organize means to furnish or make arrangements for an initiative 'orderly structure', put into working order. For you to be successful being organized is a necessary attribute. No matter how small your business, ministry, or project, to rise above failure, you must be organized.

This entails arranging your structures orderly, putting first things first, keeping records, and laying strategies among others. If you want to take a loan from any bank as a business person, the bank will want to see your financial records. This cannot be possible if you don't keep records.

Writing down your vision is the most important step towards achieving success. A written paper is better than sharp memory. When you don't write down your idea, two things are likely to happen; either you will never do what you wanted to do or you will end up doing a different thing from what you had intended to do. Nothing dies quicker than an idea in a closed mind. By writing your vision, you are simply exercising faith and God will cause it to come to pass.

Habakkuk 2:2-3

".. write the vision and make it plain upon tablets that he may run that readeth it" For the vision is yet for an appointed time, but at the end of it shall speak and not lie: though it Tarry, wait for it, because it will surely come, it will not tarry.'

Some ideas that God gives us may seem impossible for now, but nevertheless write them down. They are for a time appointed of God. Whether you have the capital for your business or not, whether you have the school fees or not, just write down your vision and keep praying for it. It is your faith that shall bring it to fulfillment. Learn to see the end from the beginning, and the far you can see God shall give to you.

Keep records

Whatever you do either in your business or ministry, keep records. Keep records of expenditure, income, achievements, and/or challenges you face. These records will help you to retrospect, reflect, and gauge yourself to see if you are making any progress.

There are people who may be willing to support you. They will require seeing where you're coming from. It also helps you to be accountable and also spend wisely. Every new idea requires sacrifice and self-discipline.

Organize yourself

Adjust yourself to a lifestyle that fits your idea. Every job has its dressing code. For example if you want to become a mechanic you can't dress like a pastor. You must adjust yourself to dressing in overalls and be ready to touch grease and oil.

Seek knowledge and understanding from experienced people on how they do their work. What are the pros and cons in that job, ministry, business, or project? Do not go in blindly or else you may never succeed in your endeavours.

Always seek to advance the skills required in your job.

*If the axe is dull and its edges unsharpened, more strength
is needed. But skill will bring success*
Ecclesiastes 10:10

Remember David did not just kill Goliath; he had
experience from killing a lion and a bear in the bushes (see
I Samuel 17:37). He had nobody to train him on how to use
weapons but he learnt the know-how through experience. In
addition to learning through experience, there are schools
that offer training on what you do or plan to do. Do not ignore
knowledge for the Bible says –

"my people are destroyed for lack of knowledge"
Hosea 4:6

Read books that talk about what you do. Iron sharpens
iron, the experience of others will help you not to fail where
they failed and succeed easily. Be ready for challenges.
John L. Mason said 'Don't ask for rain if you are afraid of
mud'. There are challenges in every success but we must fight;
don't be afraid of a day you have never seen, face it.

III. A - Act now

W. H. Murray said "Are you in earnest? Seize this minute.
Whatever you dream you can begin it. Boldness has genius,
power, and magic in it. Only engage and then the mind grows
heated. Begin and the work will be completed."
The time for action is now not tomorrow. The tomorrow
people never begin. Many people have ideas but they are still
sitting on them. They keep on saying I will start tomorrow,

and their tomorrow never comes. Others are waiting for conditions to be good to start. The conditions around you will never be good enough for you to start anything. You must fly against the wind like an eagle and the wind will help you mount up higher.

Action springs not from thought, but from a readiness for responsibility. Position yourself and be ready for responsibility. Start from scratch and keep on scratching. God has already given you what you need to begin but many find themselves saying "If only I had this, if only I were there or that.... If only I had more money... Start with what you have not what you don't have. Stop ignoring the seed that God has put in you. Don't let what you cannot do keep you from doing what you can do. True greatness consists of being great and faithful in little things. You don't start climbing a mountain from the top; you must start from the bottom and proceed to the top.

Zechariah 4:10
"For who hath despised the days of small things..."

Every great idea began small; a long journey starts with one step. People who have achieved a lot today began very small even smaller than many of us could imagine. A man in Nairobi started mixing liquid soap with a five liter container and getting only one dollar daily. Today he has his own manufacturing company. Stop sitting on your destiny. Get ready to start where you are and with what you have.

There are two great enemies of goal-setting - fear and procrastination.

Procrastination

Procrastination makes you postpone things. You hesitate in action. When you delay your plans, you delight the devil. Remember you can never succeed in anything unless you go ahead and do it before you are ready. Waiting to be ready is waiting to fail. Though it is good to prepare, some are already set; they are just procrastinating.

> 'He that observes the wind shall not sow and he that regard the cloud shall not reap."
> **Ecclesiastes 11:4**

The conditions around shall never be right for you to start. Be jealous of your time for it is your greatest treasure. Act before your idea expires. Some ideas have expiry dates. Start living your life today by doing what your dream is. Don't bury your opportunity in the grave of procrastination.

How to overcome Procrastination

When we decide to rise above failure in our lives, one of the biggest obstacles we need to overcome is procrastination. It's not that simple to take action or start something unless we develop an iron will. Though it may not be simple, it is possible. We only need to apply some simple strategies like:

I. See the end from the beginning

We often avoid tasks that we feel won't be enjoyable. Instead, take some time to think about why you will enjoy what you are going to do, even if it's simply the outcome that makes you feel inspired. State your reasons aloud, and affirm the good reasons why you should get moving. Personally, I enjoy having challenging jobs; it makes me feel good, I can release tension, and I get that great adrenaline rush! Take a few minutes to see the end result in your mind. See yourself having achieved your goal and celebrating the results. After just a few minutes of these visualizations, you may suddenly appreciate the fact that you have the idea. Now take action.

II. Encourage yourself

David knew he had to encourage himself in the Lord even when everyone was giving up.

..But David encouraged himself in the LORD his God.
1 Samuel 30:6b

I always say to myself, "I want to do this and yes I can do it", "I deserve this because my heavenly Father owns it", "I am blessed enough to live the life I want, and I refuse to be held back by my fears and negative habits", "I am capable of so much more than I've done so far", "No matter how successful I become, there is always room for improvement and growth. Just like Barack Obama, 'Yes I can, yes I can, and yes I can!'" Using affirmations like this, you will feel your resolve grow stronger, and your excitement build, and you will actually look forward to taking the action and steps that lead you down the path of success.

III. Smile to yourself

Once you've gotten started and worked on your goals for at least a week, give yourself a smile and congratulate yourself for beating procrastination. Make it a priority to applaud yourself often. Make yourself happy just like you would do to your best friend or a beloved one who is working on making their dreams come true. Become your own cheerleader!

IV. Remain Consistent

Remember that setting new goals and overcoming procrastination is a moment by moment decision. It would be great if you could make a decision and have it be so, but it doesn't usually work that way. We need to be aware of our self-defeating actions and make the effort to change them moment by moment, day by day, and week by week. Keep this in mind even when setting your goals.

Rather than setting yourself up for failure by beating your chest that you shall do this or that, and become this or that, just say "Today by God's grace, I will do this or that." Let the Lord take care of tomorrow, even though you have your goals. This makes action and success less intimidating and you won't feel so pressured to be perfect.

The Bible says in **Proverbs 16:1-3** (King James Version) –

The preparations of the heart in man, and the answer of the tongue, is from the Lord. All the ways of a man are clean in his own eyes; but the Lord weigheth the hearts

People mostly fail when they leave God out of their plans just because they have had one or two achievements. In the end, it is the power and grace of God that helps us to keep getting up again after we've stumbled or fallen.

God will strengthen our will and lead us along the path of success. So, if you have been struggling with procrastination, don't despair! Simply set yourself up for success by developing strategies that will blast your excuses right out of the water.

Today is the day to start. God knows why He gave that idea today. Obey Him not your instincts or men. He knows the way to make you succeed so follow Him.

Psalm 37:2 (King James Version)

> *The steps of a good man are ordered by the Lord: and he delighteth in His ways*

V. Look back and see if you are on track.

A good builder uses a plumb line to check if he is building in a straight line. If he does not use a plumb line he might end up with a bending wall, or the whole house may collapse.

Putting checks and balances on your way to success is very important. You get more ideas from people as well as discouragement; if you take every idea that comes your way and apply it to your original plan it may end up distorting the originality.

If you listen to criticism from people, you will never finish what you started. Always remember you are the pioneer of your dream. Let people advice you but do not allow them to influence you. People will tell you "If you would have done this, or that, or if you do this instead of that..." If you allow many voices to control you, you will get more confused and do the wrong thing. Everybody will have his own way of doing things, but remember you cannot do what everybody thinks is right. You also have your own way of doing things. Always carry on with your original ideas;

It is true that in Proverbs 11:14 the Bible says *many advices build a strong city* but you must have a filter for every advice you receive. See which one is good for you and which one is not. Take the right ones and ignore the rest. Advice and people's opinions should not change the original picture of what you wanted but they should add value to it.

In the same manner, looking back does not mean dwelling in the past. It simply means comparing where you are with where you were to see where you are going. Learn from your yesterday's failures but do not dwell on them. Do not dwell even on the successes of yesterday.

Your life is in the future not in the past. Yesterday was your training, today is your graduation and projection day, tomorrow is full of opportunities and it is determined by the choices you make today. Your tomorrow's success is not determined by yesterday but by today.

Some people allow their past to hold them back. You can never plan the future by dwelling on the past. The past is gone. We cannot change the past but we can change the future by learning from the past and making right choices today. The future only frightens those who prefer living in the past.

A driver who does not use his side mirror either knocks other vehicles or takes the wrong courses on the road. The side mirror will tell you when to stop, accelerate, and overtake. Both the side mirrors and front focus are equally important when driving. Looking back helps us to avoid repeating mistakes. If you did not qualify for that tender, it is important to see where you went wrong and work on your mistakes and weaknesses. This helps you rise above failure or disqualifications in the next tender. Correct your past by living right today and get better results tomorrow.

VI. Set New Goals

After the first victory, never relax and when you get to the top, work on staying there. We live in a world of great competition. People are dreaming every day; piracy is all over, nationally and internationally.

You may come up with a very good idea and begin working on it, but as soon as people know what you are doing or planning to do they may take your idea and run before you. It is rather unfortunate that originality of some big ideas has been from common people who never enjoy the success of their ideas. Some young people start great ideas. But due to lack of capital to start off, these ideas are taken by people who have financial ability and who pretend to be the pioneers of such ideas. This makes the rightful owners of the idea never to be known or even heard of.

There is a need to protect the upcoming entrepreneurs who have great visions and ideas.

You who is reading this book, need to therefore set new goals even after the first one. Have ideas on top of other ideas. This will help you to always be ahead of others. Never think you are the only player in the field. You have many competitors. Always be innovative, be creative. You have God's mind, you were created for creativity. Your new ideas are an indicator of your potential to staying great. While your eyes look for opportunity, let your heart long for God's time. The win-win approach will only apply here with some checks. If I have the idea and you have the money, then we can go the win-win way, as long as we play as per the rules. You should bring the money while I bring the idea, then we become equal partners of the business.

Don't let anyone take advantage of you because they have financed your idea. Your idea is as equally important as their money. To succeed always renovate your dream by setting new goals.

Chapter Three

Acquire Knowledge & Information

Information is the currency of today's world

Acquire Knowledge & Information

Information has become the world's currency. Those who control information have become the most powerful people on the planet.

Information Technology (IT) is transforming the world. For us to succeed in the 21st century we must adjust to new technologies. I may not be an information guru but I have realised that we are living in the Information Age, a time when we must adjust to new technologies and that the man who has information is the king.

You should never be one of those people frozen by indecision because of the lack of enough information to make a safe choice or decision. I've come to trust intuition and experience as important allies when faced with dealing with any challenge. As someone who wants to succeed, whether in your career, profession, business, or church ministry, you must be well informed.

Today's school system is a 'get the right answer system'. Many graduates from colleges and even universities join companies with this kind of mentality - 'As long as I'm doing it right, it's alright with me.' This hinders their growth as an individual and also the growth of the company or institution that they are working for.

One day I met the Operations Director of one of the top financial services companies in Nairobi. They had just launched an online share trading services product. She had plans to expand to other Kenyan Diaspora, and we discussed her expansion plans to the African Market. She expressed to me her great expansion plans and the challenge she had. She mentioned her disappointments from her junior managers whom she could not rely on to head their new branches in other countries.

When I asked her why she was disappointed by the team of managers working with her, she said, Out of the thirty whom we have trained on the new product, only three have challenged me and I have already promoted them to head three new branches in different countries.

She simply meant that only the three were willing to research and get more information on the new product. They could at least challenge her by finding solutions and fixing loopholes which show up in a new product as it goes into the market.

What your employer might be looking for in order to promote you is based more on your ability to get more information than on what you do. Instead of you relying on your boss for a solution in your promotion, he/she expects you to search for information that will provide a solution. As you rise through the ranks of management, the higher you go, the more informed you need to become in order to lead others through the wilderness of situations where no one has gone before. Information is an extremely valuable asset that should always be sought and used as a manager's most important tool for decision-making.

You benefit from gaining knowledge and applying that knowledge as a skill in your work. You become confident and sure of yourself when confronted with problems when you are informed.

Being treated by others as a knowledgeable or skilled person is a great reward and a great motivator especially when it comes from your seniors.

When I got a job with the bank, I only had experience in real estate. I joined the bank as a Relationship Manager in Housing and mortgages. Not coming from the banking sector, I had to learn a lot about banking. To match the challenge that was laid ahead of me, I had to gather information from every source.

Ignorance is never an excuse. I managed to successfully go through my six months' probation. I was promoted to the position of the Manager in charge of Mortgages and Asset products. The responsibilities became more and more.

There were more educated people in the bank, more experienced and longer serving staff than I was but I was picked. All these I attributed them first to God and then to the ability to gather information and knowledge besides my education level. Both knowledge and information are important to your success.

The thirst for knowledge is a driving force among all great men and women of today, and you can be among them. You must seek to be well informed in the area of your operations and beyond as this will easily put you in the limelight and on the forefront, whether you are employed, in business, or in politics.

For Preachers

When I first started preaching, out of ignorance I thought preaching is just applying a lot of force and having a rough voice. I thought I just needed to read one scripture and base my sermon on it as I had heard many preachers on TV and radio do. With time I realised that the people who come to church need more than a scripture, and they needed more than the Bible. Some of these people have read through the Bible time and again and just reading the Bible to them is not enough. A good number of them are graduates from reputable universities and are working in senior positions; they do not need noise but knowledge. This challenge pushed me to look for a way to be ahead of those I lead and preach to, and that was by being informed.

Knowledge is power when it comes to making a point either in an argument or in an attempt to persuade others to believe in your sermon.

Arguments are won by people who have the facts. They are won when the opponent cannot punch holes in what is presented. The person with less knowledge of a subject is usually the one who presents an argument in which the opponent can easily punch holes.

Preaching is no different from the above quote; we need to be extra informed than the people we speak to or else our audience will punch holes to our preaching.

You can acquire knowledge from college and lecturers, but you must search for information in order to be informed. It is not enough to rely only on the knowledge offered by the set curriculum in schools; seek information and understanding. The right information in the right place just changes your life.

We are living in the age of Information Technology which is now a key to success in any business and a requirement for you as an individual. Churches are not left out in this; any preacher who is not well versed in computer literacy is risking being counted as 'old-school'. There are software packages which have been created to enable preachers to best study the Bible. Software like e-sword has all Bibles translations, commentaries, and dictionaries. The best way to forego ignorance is to have knowledge in the latest information.

Students need information too

It's sometimes disturbing when you look at what our pupils in school are taught even today in the 21st Century. The world is changing and advancing too fast but it takes decades for schools to adjust their curriculum. It is sixteen years since I left primary school. The same stuff we were taught then is practically the same that a pupil in 2011 is being taught. Teaching pupils about provinces when Kenya is under a new constitutional dispensation which brought in counties to replace provinces is totally wasting their mental space.

Institutions are already moving from paper to paperless transactions. The computer programs we are using today are much advanced than those of the last decade. Everything is moving very fast. The weather patterns that we were taught about in the 20th century have drastically changed due to global warming.

The kinds of people our schools are producing are but a very dull and uninformed generation which is preparing to step in to a very fast-changing world. They are products of what you may call the 'get-the-right-answer' system where students study only to pass their exams. This is not wrong in itself, but teachers have to bring up an informed generation of leaders from schools and colleges. Take away the unnecessary subjects and bring in others which connect the students to the current world. Educate them on how to approach life with an open mind; that they may find a job or go to business.

They should be like a multifaceted tool which will never be idle, but can find something to do anywhere, at anytime. Expose the students and pupils to every reading material that can add value to their life or more to change the way they see life. If I had read Stephen Covey's book, *The Seven habits of Highly Effective People,* when I was young, I would not be where I am today.

To be informed is more than just getting a high grade. Expose students to information and they will be able to make informed choices. The cry of joblessness will then get an antidote.

Always keep a Note book

For those already working, whether in business, a church minister, a senior manager, a junior manager, or anyone else, acquired information must be recorded. In my operations as a pastor, I have learnt that congregants need a note book in a church Service to take notes of the sermons. No sharp memory is sharp enough to remember all the year's sermons, so most of your time in church will go to waste when you forget. As a pastor, I have to record every revelation that I get so that I don't forget. Our minds have so many things to think about that they cannot record everything important that you hear.

I was very poor in taking notes because I trusted my memory. However this started failing me when I started handling much information. When I first became a manager in a company, I thought I was overworking but I realised I was not using the art of recording information. My then director told me never to come to her meetings without a note book. This helped me ease the strain of trying to remember everything when a crisis occurred in the company. I only pulled out my notebook and I would get what I wanted.

She also taught me how to prepare a to-do list. She could call me for what looked like a very informal meeting, but as we discussed I learnt to be very sensitive to every suggestion she made. This ability to gather information brings us success and makes us work easier.

Protect your information

The digitization of our world is something we expected, understand, and even demand. For many of us and for many institutions, financial records, contact lists, transactions, and books are all stored online. However, for all its ease, convenience, and speed, the digital part of our life is not without its dangers. In this case, a lost flash drive, or a server crash could be catastrophic.

Those who still cling to paper records and documents, always have a backup. But, with so much of our lives already tied up in gigabytes, RAM, and servers, what can be done to protect our digital lives? Backup is the answer.

Backing-up data is a common computer support suggestion. Backing-up your digital files to a USB, external hard drive, or offsite data center is a great idea. But you can find even more security in keeping hard copies – on paper - of your essential documents.

Be Protected - With so much of our lives online and digitized, it's vital that we always think of our computers, websites, and other digital 'homes'. We don't leave our physical homes unprotected, and the same should be true for the digital ones. Internet security software to guard against malware, spyware, and viruses, is important as a smoke detector or an alarm system in your office is.

Keep your own records - Banks, financial institutions, and other institutions face the same online dangers as you - a server crash, a virus, or a security breach can wipe out data. Keep your own records, either by printing out information, by recording things on your own, or by sending important information to your email address.

Be redundant - Never trust any one single digital or online source to preserve everything. Make multiple copies in multiple locations. Use several different online storage sites for your documents. Just be sure.

Be prepared - If you do face a data crisis, be prepared. Know what's on all of your devices, including file types, names, and how important each bit of information is. This will help prioritise your data recovery needs, and might help save your most important data.

The digital world is making inroads every day, most of them welcome. But now that we're facing an increasingly online existence, it's vital to know all the ways you can make sure that the digital world works for and not against you and your institution.

Power of Knowledge

John F. Kennedy once said 'The greater our knowledge increases the more our ignorance unfolds'

> **Hosea 4:6** (KJV) —*My people are destroyed for lack of knowledge: because thou hast rejected knowledge, I will also reject thee, that thou shalt be no priest to me: seeing thou hast forgotten the law of thy God, I will also forget thy children.*

Knowledge is information in use or in action. According to the Hebrew dictionary, knowledge is defined as - cunning, [ig-] norantly, know (-ledge), [un-] awares (wittingly).

According to Turban, —Knowledge is information that has been organised and analyzed to make it understandable and applicable to problem-solving or decision-making.

Knowledge is also the cumulative stock of information and skills derived from use of information by the recipient, according to Burton-Jones.

Knowledge has also been defined as that which is known and is an essentially human form of information. By selecting and analyzing data, we can produce information, and by selecting and combining information, we... generate knowledge.

Tacit and Explicit Knowledge

Tacit knowledge is such that is inherently indescribable. Tacit knowledge is gathered by senses, from experience and intuition, for example during interaction with people. Explicit knowledge on the other hand is that which has been coded or written down and is accessible to everyone.

For you as an individual to benefit from your knowledge, it is important for you to convert the tacit knowledge you have to explicit knowledge. It is always better to keep a written note than to trust a sharp memory. You save the knowledge from getting lost, and you can easily refer to your note book or piece of paper in future. Those who use diaries, notebooks, or other written material should never throw them away.

For institutions and companies, it is more than necessary to use all the means possible to decode the tacit knowledge which the employees have. Otherwise when employees retire or change their jobs they take the tacit knowledge they had with them, and this can put the company into a lapse. The person who takes over that position will have no reference of where to start. It will not be easy to know the WIPs (work in progress) of the company.

Tacit knowledge is a human centered asset which belongs to the individual. Knowledge in the tacit state is easily lost when employees go on leave or resign from the organization; but when it is codified into explicit knowledge it is an asset that belongs to the organization. I have seen office assistants, accountants, and engineers who go on leave but have to be recalled before their time is over just because no one knows how they do this or that in the entire organization. Some of this employees work without leave or a break just because no one else knows or can do what they do. It should never be so for an organization which is working on being successful. Being knowledgeable is the first step in becoming skilled and then confident. It is one of the powers of a champion. It means you are aware of your surroundings, you remember and understand things you learn, and you know how to perform various related tasks. But achieving that goal can be a challenge due to outside forces and your own destructive attitude. Knowledge is useful across all sectors and works, whether you are employed, a business person, a preacher, an artist, or a farmer. Your effectiveness in what you do is tied up in your ability to source for knowledge in your area of operation and the ability to apply it as well. Knowledge must be worked, unlike wisdom which we are told to ask from our heavenly Father.

> **James 1:5** (KJV) —*If any of you lack wisdom, let him ask of God, that giveth to all men liberally, and upbraideth not; and it shall be given him*

You benefit from gaining knowledge and applying that knowledge as a skill. You become confident or sure of yourself when confronted with problems. . The thirst for knowledge is a driving force among all great men and women.

The journey to gaining knowledge starts by a way of thinking toward knowledge. This can be practiced through being observant, being curious, taking interest in many subjects, being well-rounded, trying to apply your knowledge, learning to think logically, reading rapidly, having a good memory, creating analogies, being creative, and thinking "outside the box".

Among the many ways of gaining knowledge, there are the common ones - reading, observation, and listening.

I. Reading

It has been said that if you want to hide anything from a Kenyan, hide it in a book. I challenge everyone to adopt a reading culture because most of the problems we have, have solutions in books. If I developed it then anyone else can. There is no successful person I know of who is not a reader. You cannot lead if you don't read. Reading inspires you so you don't expire, and above all it equips you for success.

One of the most important ways to gain knowledge in the modern world is by reading. You can witness the experiences and thoughts that people have documented throughout the ages through reading. Reading can include the newspapers, magazines, work- or school-related books, fiction, and books on subjects of interest. One must-read book is the Bible, which is the word of God and a life-giver. Reading fiction can not only get you involved in the story, but is also a source of useful facts and representations of how people act and think. Books and magazine articles can also teach. You should not only read about things you are interested in, but also be curious enough to look into new material and different subjects.

There are millions and millions of books written throughout the world in every language and on almost any topic imaginable. Whatever problem you are facing must have been faced by somebody else before, and its solution is likely to have been preserved in the form of a book. If you are serious about gaining knowledge on a topic, then read any book, magazine, article, etc, that you can lay your hands on related to that topic. Read as much as you can.

What to read

When you are reading you need to separate the wheat' from the chaff.' Alongside useful information there exists a large quantity of useless or even incorrect information. Even within a useful text, there may be extraneous information on which you just don't need to spend time on. Speed-reading and skim-reading are useful skills to help decide what you should read. Good reading strategies help you to read in a very efficient way. Using these strategies, you aim to benefit from your reading with the minimum effort.

There are different strategies to read intelligently. Knowing what you want to know, the first thing to ask yourself is:

- Why you are reading this book. Are you reading with a purpose or just for pleasure?
- What do you want to know after reading it?

Once you know this, you can examine the text to see whether it is going to move you towards your goal.

An easy way of doing this is to look at the introduction and the chapter headings if the book is open. The introduction should let you know to whom the book is targeted, and what it seeks to achieve. Chapter headings will give you an overall view of the structure of the subject. If the book is sealed, read the back page or Google-up the book and read the introduction online.

Ask yourself whether the book meets your needs. Ask yourself if it assumes too much or too little knowledge. If the book isn't ideal, would it be better to find a better one? Don't just read for the sake of reading.

Knowing how deeply to study the material: Where you only need the shallowest knowledge of the subject, you can skim (speed-reading) material. Here you read only chapter headings, introductions and summaries.

If you need a moderate level of information on a subject, then you can scan the text. Here you read the chapter introductions and summaries in detail. You may then speed read the contents of the chapters, picking out and understanding key words and concepts. At this level of looking at the document it is worth paying attention to diagrams and graphs.

Only when you need detailed knowledge of a subject is it worth studying the text. Here it is best to skim the material first to get an overview of the subject. This gives you an understanding of its structure, into which you can fit the detail gained from a full reading of the material.

Active Reading: When you are reading a document in detail, it often helps if you highlight, underline, and annotate it as you go on. This emphasizes information in your mind, and helps you to review important points later.

A friend took a book from my library and complained that I had messed it up by commenting on the margins. I told him that I had bought the book to read and understand not just read. Highlighting a book helps to keep your mind focused on the material and stops it from wandering. This is obviously only something to do if you own the book. If you own it and you don't want to mess the pages, then it may be worth photocopying information. You can then read and mark the photocopies. If you are worried about destroying the material, ask yourself how much your investment of time is worth. If the benefit you get by active reading reasonably exceeds the value of the book, then the book is disposable.

Study different sorts of material: Different sorts of documents hold information in different places and in different ways. They have different depths and breadths of coverage. By understanding the layout of the material you are reading, you can extract useful information much more efficiently.

Reading is an important way to gain knowledge. You can get books from the library or bookstore. You can access articles, essays, and lessons over the internet on sites such as Google, Amazon, and Wikipedia, as well as government and other public portals.

You must be willing to spend in order to gain knowledge.

II. Observation

Children especially learn by observation. Watching what others do is an important way to gain knowledge. Adults also need to use this technique.

Observe how others do business, how your boss does things, how your pastor preaches. Pride causes people not to observe others in the way they do things. If you are a singer, you don't want to sit and learn from others, and as a preacher you lack the humility to observe how successful pastors run their churches. It is the same with business people and professionals. Always leave a learning space in your life.

No wonder Jesus said we must be like little children for us to inherit the Kingdom of heaven. It is not only so with the Kingdom; for you to gain skills to succeed in anything, observation is an important skill.

Mathew 18: 3-4 *And (Jesus) said, —Verily I say unto you, except ye be converted, and become as little children, ye shall not enter into the kingdom of heaven. Whosoever therefore shall humble himself as this little child, the same is greatest in the kingdom of heaven.*

Looking is not seeing

As we learn the power of information and knowledge in the art of success, we ought to know the art of observation.

Meaning is lost when all we do is look at something. To see something means to understand it in a deeper way.

Seeing is a transformative experience - it suggests action in that it promotes feeling, thinking and responding toward something. Passively looking at something however means noticing without acting. When we open our eyes, mind and heart to the world around us, we become alive to it. In a culture saturated with visual messages, our eyes, and by extension our minds and hearts, have become numb and anesthetized to the desire to seek out the deeper meanings of the things we are exposed to.

Observation begins with immersing ourselves in the textures and tones of life. Observation requires us to immerse ourselves in looking and listening without passing judgment on the impressions we collect. We must free ourselves from the biases, preferences and prejudices we hold toward our subjects.

The glaring contrast between seeing and looking at the world around us is immense; it is fateful. Everything in our society seems to conspire against our inborn human gift of seeing.

Learning to observe people, places, and activities in the world can make us knowledgeable, good communicators, writers, and good leaders.

We have become addicted to merely looking at things and beings. The more we regress from seeing to looking at the world through the ever-more-perfected machinery of viewfinders, TV tubes, VCRs, microscopes, stereoscopes – the less we see, the more numbed we become to the joy and the pain of being alive, and the further estranged we become from ourselves and all others.

Learn to observe without judging, without letting thoughts intrude between you and the object. Observation is a process of immersing ourselves in listening and looking more carefully. When you see a sunset or a landscape and say, —How beautiful, you are not immersed in it, and will notice only part of what you might otherwise have seen.

Whatever field you want to gain knowledge in, there must be many who have enough experience in that field. So make use of this valuable source of information by learning from the experience, accomplishments, mistakes, and expertise of others. Study carefully and associate with people who are experts in the field you want to gain knowledge about. Knowledge is like money. The more you get, the more you crave.

III. Listening

> Proverbs 1:5 '*A wise man will hear, and will increase learning; and a man of understanding shall attain unto wise counsels*'

Listening is another way of gaining knowledge. Listening to what other people say, listening to teachers, other preachers, instructions, and tutorials from your boss or professors is a good example of this.

The art of listening

If you listen with your eyes, your ears, and your mind you will always get the information you need. You must listen to hear, so that you may get the information being conveyed by the speaker.

You can use the following skills to be a good listener both on the telephone and in person:

- Always be prepared to take notes when necessary. That means having writing tools readily available.
- Develop the desire to listen. You must accept the fact that listening to others is your strongest weapon. Given the opportunity, the other person will tell you everything you need to know. If this doesn't create desire, I don't know what will.
- Always let the other person do most of the talking. Try to listen 70% of the time and talk 30% of the time.
- Don't interrupt. There is always the temptation to interrupt so you can tell the other person something you

think is vitally important. It isn't, so don't. When you are about to speak, ask yourself if it is really necessary.

- Learn active listening. It's not enough that you're listening to someone; you want to be sure that they know you're listening. Active listening is the art of communicating to the other person that you're hearing their every word.
- Ask for clarification if needed. This will clear up any misunderstanding you have.
- Get used to 'listening' for non-verbal messages i.e. body language. The other person may be communicating with you via body language. You need to decode the message. Listen by using the ears to hear the message, the eyes to read body language (when listening in person), the mind to visualize the person speaking (when on the telephone), and intuition to determine what the speaker is actually saying.
- Ask a question...then shut up. This is a foolproof way to listen. Think of yourself as an interviewer – Barbara Walters! She listens and questions and so should you.
- Be physically and mentally present in the moment.
- Establish rapport by following the leader.
- Match the momentum, tone of voice, body language, and words used by the speaker.
- Please use common sense when matching. If the speaker is yelling, don't do the same because it will make the situation worse.

In a conversation, many people don't really listen to what the other person is saying. Instead, they are thinking of what they want to say next. And so they hear mostly what they want to hear, not what the other person is trying to communicate to them. Many conflicts can be resolved easily if we learn how to listen.

In my marketing and sales experience for the last eleven years, I have learnt that the key to success in selling, as it is in negotiating, is keeping your mouth shut and listening to what people have to say. I have discovered that my sales prospects will tell me everything I need to know in order to make the sale if I just keep my mouth shut long enough. If I try to make a flowery presentation, chances are high that I may lose the sale. But if I let them tell me what their problems are, they will buy any idea from me.

Being a good listener takes discipline. If you can train yourself to keep your mouth shut most of the time, you will be a great listener, a great learner, and a great negotiator.

When you were a child you may have listened to stories or things your parents explained. Later, in conversations with friends, you gained knowledge from what they told you. As an adult, there are many times that listening is a source of knowledge. People that prefer to talk and don't care to listen will often lose out on important information and knowledge.

For those who are in college, besides reading, listening to your teacher or professor as he lectures on a subject is a major source of knowledge. Another source comes from discussions on the subject with other students. This can also be true at work, where a superior or talented person may provide useful information or instructions regarding your job.

We also gain a fair amount of knowledge by listening to people talk on the radio or TV. At the very least, you can get the news. Unfortunately, much of the information gained in comedy shows is either useless or even promotes negative behavior. This is where many people have failed; when they spend most of their time watching movies, comedies, and non-valuable programs on TV. Try and spend most of your time learning something new even on TV.

Listening is a powerful way of gaining knowledge. You can learn through conversations, in school, or at work, and also through the radio and TV.

When you lose your hearing, you lose contact with people just like when you lose your vision, you lose contact with things.

Get the diamond from the dirt

They say knowledge is power but, if that were the case, academics would rule the world. Knowledge in itself is not power; rather the application of knowledge is where power lies. They say a little knowledge is a dangerous thing. Well too much learning without applying it can lead to paralysis and a lack of decisive, timely action.

In this world, success is about finding diamonds in the dirt. Time is the diamond in the dirt of knowledge. We are constantly trying to find time.

Knowledge is only useful if we act on what we know, so we need to balance the time we spend knowing with the time we spend doing.

Companies, churches, and all institutions should be well versed with Knowledge Management (KM) as well as Information Management (IM).

Success of institutions is much determined by whether they understand the power of information and knowledge. A piece of paper with information is very important. Not all papers should be thrown to the dustbin. The conclusion of this chapter is; you too can make it, success is not for some people, but for anyone who is willing to learn its art and put it into action.

Chapter Four

Be Creative

The ability to imagine or invent something new

Be Creative

A simple definition of creativity is _the ability to imagine or invent something new.' Creativity is not the ability to create out of nothing (only God did that), but it is the ability to generate new ideas by combining, changing, or reapplying existing ideas. They may be simple but brilliant things that no one seems to have thought of yet.

Everyone has a substantial creative ability, from children, young people, to working class people. All that's needed to be creative is to make a commitment to creativity and to make the time for it.

Creativity will keep you at the top in anything that you do. New ideas can make your star shine anywhere. You may not have money to implement your new ideas, but creative ideas have a trend of financing themselves.

We do a lot of things today the same way we did them yesterday, and then we create a habit. Habits can be helpful, but a habit can also shut out creativity. We become more creative precisely at those times of extreme frustration when yesterday's habit solutions don't solve today's problems.

Creativity can also be brought about by passion for your work. Passion is that great feeling of excitement, joy, and intensity that you get when you truly love what you're doing. If we go through our days feeling bored or uninspired or stressed, we lose the passion for our work and so the power of creativity is quenched. On the other hand, doing something with passion and joy brings forth energy that literally makes us get creative in what we do. Most of us go through our daily routine on an autopilot, and we don't make an effort to feel interested in what we're doing. Rather than mindlessly going to work, make it an enjoyable experience. Put on some good music and sing along. Repeat empowering affirmations to lift your mood. During your daily routine, pay more attention to the things you do, and find a way to make them interesting. If you take a greater interest in everything around you, everything will seem much more interesting.

Every step in my career has been brought about by God's grace and creativity. Not looking at the return but just loving the job will bring returns automatically in the future. This way, when you fail, you will be able to rise up and stay above failure by being more creative than ever.

Creativity is the mother of invention, no matter where and why we are becoming creative. Creativity is not just a collection of intellectual abilities. It is also a personality type, a way of thinking and living. Although creative people tend to be unconventional, they share common traits. For example, creative thinkers are confident, independent, and risk-takers. They are perceptive and have good intuition. They display flexible, original thinking. They dare to differ, make waves, challenge traditions, and bend a few rules.

We can enhance our creativity by associating with certain types of behavior and reasoning. This doesn't mean that a simple formula can be derived, or that one technique will work for everybody, or that success is guaranteed. But certain steps seem likely to increase your creativity.

i. Being restless

To be creative, begin by conditioning yourself to be restless and uneasy about the status quo. Don't overlook the familiar things just because you've seen them so often. Rather make yourself even more aware of them, and then change how you do them slightly. If you start selling with a call, to an appointment, then a follow-up, try changing your ordinary selling formula. If you start preaching by reading the Bible then prayer and preaching, try something else and don't fear people seeing you as weird. At least change your routine once and see the result. Breaking your routine will help you invent an improved process or idea.

ii. See things differently

To be creative, see things differently, from a new angle, from another scale of time or distance, or from the perspective of someone with a different background. Explore things beyond the bounds of your expertise.

If you have a glimpse of a good idea, preserve it by writing it down immediately. Then take your own time, think about the idea through and classify it as either worthy or insignificant. You can then revise, revise, and revise your idea again and again until you know the pros and cons in it. Consider your idea a rough draft that needs to be polished by a few cycles through the 'idea-processor' as Dr. Davis calls it.

iii. Creative-thinking time

For you to be creative, schedule regular times for creative thinking. The city's traffic is tedious for those who reside here. The morning and evening journey to and from the office may be a tiresome one whether by commuter bus or train, but you can dedicate the journey as a scheduled time for creative thinking, for dreaming, for envisioning what might happen, for devising imaginative solutions.

Many of the innovations I have made were derived either in the morning or evening journey to and from the office. Don't allow your mind to be occupied with negative thoughts and the day's stresses; rather allow yourself it to be creative.

You can also get creative while listening to or watching news or some interesting movie. Out of what people do, either from their mistakes or their good work you can get better and creative ideas. You must learn to always be ahead of your competitors through creativity.

Barriers to Creativity

i. Experience

Although experience is often valuable, it can be a liability if in a search for creative ideas. Herman Kahn called experience "educated incapacity". If you operate always on your experience, you will soon expire. The world is revolving and it will take creative minds to stay at the top of their careers, ministries, and businesses. Creativity made Safaricom introduce a first-ever in the world - mobile money transfer system.

Once you begin a new idea, competitors will rise to challenge you. If you stick to your experience and stop being creative, you will soon be overtaken by your competitors. Creativity makes competitors come after you but never to overtake you.

ii. Assumptions

For years, the banks operated under the assumption that their competition was from other banks only. No doubt this affected and constrained their creative efforts. However, the unexpected popularity of sending money using just a mobile phone took them by surprise. They tried to challenge the innovation but it was an unstoppable creative idea. That's what happens when you assume things.

You can never enjoy monopoly of ideas in this current world. It happened in the years of invention but now players in every industry including church ministries have increased. Some are genuine others are pirates. Some brands stayed at the top as the best until creativity got them behind others. Never rest in creativity. Think and think every day on how to improve yourself and your job then you will be able to rise above failure and stay ahead of the competition.

iii. The "right answer" syndrome

Most school systems are better at turning out automatons of students who can memorize and parrot the right answer. They are not experts at turning out people who can think and invent new answers. Our education system especially in Kenya is a get-the-right-answer system. When you look for the right answer, you only look for what someone else already invented. There is no innovation in the new generations of graduates being released from colleges. This is an already failing system.

For creative minds, failing while looking for your own answer is the right formula. You don't follow a formula which was used by anybody else. This is the reason why many of our young people go to school - to later get employed. Every single year our streets are filled with jobless people looking for employment. They have no know-how of getting their own ideas and earning from them.

If you want to shine your star amidst many other stars, you must get out of the known way of doing things, not fearing to fail but willing to learn from your failures. For creative minds, failures are not known as failures but lessons of life. You must be willing to learn many of those lessons.

Thomas Edison refused to be in the get-the-right-answer category when a friend suggested that his attempts to develop an electric storage battery were a failure since he had tried thousands of times without success, Edison replied: *I've got a lot of results! I know several thousand things that won't work."*

Barriers of creativity in a company/organization

Creativity in companies and institutions dies when the managers:

- Always pretend to know more than anybody else.
- Police their employees by every procedural means.
- Have their professionally-trained staff members do technicians' work for long periods of time.

- Erect the highest possible barrier between commercial decision-makers and technical staff.
- Don't speak to employees on a personal level, except when announcing raises.
- Become the exclusive spokesmen for everything for which they are responsible.
- Say —Yes to new ideas but do nothing about them.
- Call many meetings.
- Put every new idea through channels.
- Worry about the budget.
- Cultivate the not-invented-here syndrome.

Ways of approaching creativity

i. Forget everything you know

Understand that every act of creation is first of all an act of destruction. For you to allow creativity into your mind, assume to forget everything you know and allow yourself to find new ways of doing things. Let your mind be renewed.

> Romans 12:2 *Do not conform to the pattern of this world, but be transformed by the renewing of your mind. Then you will be able to test and approve what God's will is—his good, pleasing and perfect will.*

Our God is a creative God and He created us with the ability to create. The earth was empty with animals, vegetation, and water filling the better part of the earth. Through the creative mind of people, the earth has developed to a better social place to live in today. This creativity should never stop. You have your role to play in the creation of the earth.

Do not grow old by stopping your mind from being renewed. Refuse familiarity, it kills innovation and as people grow older, they become prisoners of familiarity

Familiarity kills invention. For you to be creative you must destroy the familiarity of everything you know about your job. People are prisoners of familiarity until innovation comes. Before Safaricom innovated the M-Pesa mobile phone money transfer system people were prisoners to messengers in sending money locally, where so many people lost their money to untrustworthy, scrupulous messengers.

ii. Remember everything you know!

After the first act of destruction, you are left with a rich reservoir of bits and pieces of information, a vast storehouse of unconnected facts and fantasies, thoughts and ideas. Just like the words in a dictionary, they do nothing until you select and assemble them into a coherent whole.

The value of these pieces was expressed by Nobel laureate Albert Szent-Gyorgyi: "Discovery consists of looking at the same thing as everyone else and thinking something different." More than likely, the pieces of a problem you're looking at are the same pieces that others are looking at.

The pieces are the means to the end, but they are valueless as they stand. Thus the key to a better idea is "thinking something different."

iii. Rearrange everything you know!

Now look for new relationships among the pieces, new ways of assembling them. Edwin Land made a new combination of his images of camera and darkroom. New answers come from new arrangements of information. With all the possible combinations of information, it would be presumptuous to say your answer to a problem is the right one. You might say it's one good answer, or better than existing answers, but to unequivocally call it "best" shows more ignorance than judgment to creativity.

When you're trying to solve a problem, to create ideas, or just to do your job, the last thing you should do is to try to invent one perfect idea. Instead, develop as many ideas as you can, then pick and choose among them. Some people call them 'plan B'.

While creativity can be simple, that doesn't mean it's painless. It is not easy; it has a price to pay.

Awaken the creative mind in you

3 John 1:2 Beloved, I pray that you may prosper in all things and be in health, just as your soul prospers

A healthy soul (well fed with God's word and latest information) allows you to receive the images or pictures of possibilities that God shows each and every person, pictures of creativity which comes from imagination. These images are superimposed onto the creative mind of man.

Most people won't allow God to give them creative thoughts until they are confronted with an obstacle or need.

God is constantly growing the creative mind of man. If you have ever said in your heart; *What if,* or *I wonder,* or *I think that might work,* then you are beginning to operate under the creative mind.

If you have ever heard someone say to you, —It has never been done that way before, or —That will never work, or even —Who do you think you are? Those words may be an indication that you have received an inspired creative idea. Every creative thought will benefit more than just the one who receives it.

Examples of creativity

The Netherlands creative story

Real creativity is seen in the story of the Netherlands. The country of the Netherlands was suitable only for grazing sheep due to the fact that during some seasons of the year the land would flood or become extremely water logged. By 1100 A.D., the sea level started to rise and began to also flood the coastal villages. To correct the ocean's invasion, the people created dams to keep the water from encroaching upon their homes and businesses. Eventually they realised that if they could hold the water back, they could also regain lost land from the water. Because of the increase of the population of the Netherlands, the Dutch lords and royalty decided to build dykes offshore capturing the seawater and draining it back into the ocean leaving new dry land. As they drained the water, they uncovered rich, fertile land. Even to this day, the Dutch from time to time will add more land by building dykes and draining the seawater.

The Dutch are now experts at conquering the ocean. Some residents can easily find seashells in their backyards. Today more than half of the Netherlands is below sea level. Often old war artifacts such as mines, sunken warships, and shot-down war planes are uncovered. Just imagine what Holland would look like if the Dutch had never awakened their creative minds for a solution. The Dutch show us that you are conquered only when you stop being innovative. If you never quit, your creative imagination will make a way for victory.

Gillette's innovation

When King Camp Gillette's home burned in the Chicago Fire of 1871, he was forced to become a traveling salesman in order to support his family. While working, he met a man by the name of William Painter, the inventor of the disposable Crown Cork bottle cap, who told Gillette that *'A successful invention was one that was purchased over and over by satisfied customers.'*

Years passed while Gillette tried to discover that truly genuine idea, but without success. Then suddenly in 1895 while shaving, Gillette had a brilliant idea. A razor with a safe, inexpensive, and disposable blade flashed into his mind. 'This was the beginning of the disposable movement, which we presently enjoy. Now we not only have disposable razors, but also disposable cameras, disposable napkins, and we can't forget disposable diapers,' Tracey Armstrong emphasizes.

How many times has some great and brilliant idea passed through your mind without you doing anything about bringing it to life? It took six years for the Gillette razor to evolve. Technical expert after technical expert tried to discourage Gillette, telling him it would be impossible to develop steel that was hard, thin, and inexpensive enough in order to commercialize the disposable razor blade. Finally, he found one man who was willing to try and who succeeded in 1903 — William Nickerson.

King Camp Gillette was someone who did not know the meaning of the word *quit*. He became the inventor of the first disposable razor then known as the 'Safety Razor' which was patented on November 15, 1904.

Off and running, the Gillette Safety Razor Company began operation in south Boston, and sales continued to grow steadily. The U.S. Government issued Gillette safety razors to its entire armed forces during World War I because recent studies in that day showed that shaving was hygienic for the soldiers in the field. Some 3.5 million razors and 32 million blades were put into military hands, and in doing so, the entire nation was converted to the Gillette safety razor.

That creative imagination in your mind that you have allowed to blow past may very well be the next truly original idea that the world or your company has been waiting for. The power of creativity is in you, you have the Spirit of God and you are created in His own image. He stopped on the sixth day of creation and gave you and me the power to rule and have dominion. Make where you are better than you found it by awakening the creative mind in you.

Chapter Five

Be Positive

There is a thinking stuff from which all things are made

Be Positive

There is a thinking from which all things are made, and which, in its original state, permeates, penetrates, and fills the interspaces of the universe. A thought in this substance produces the thing that is imaged by the thought. A person can form things in his thought, and, by impressing his thought upon formless substance, can cause the thing he thinks about to be created.
Wallace D. Wattles

Positive thinking is a mental attitude that admits into the mind thoughts, words and images that are conductive to growth, expansion, and success. It is a mental attitude that is in expectation of good and favourable results. Positive-minded people anticipate happiness, joy, health, and a successful outcome of every situation and action. Whatever their mind expects, it finds. They also trust and know that they will make the right decisions and the right choices. Since they expect it – their minds and their subconscious minds find a way to make things happen and stay above failure. This is the power of having a positive-thinking mindset.

Positive thinking is a practice and it requires that you have a certain mental attitude. When you have a positive mindset you automatically have positive thoughts and you continually recite positive affirmations. With a positive-thinking mindset you almost instantly find answers to even the most complex problems and challenges in life.

Before you can develop a positive thinking pattern you first have to realize that positive thinking is not something you do randomly. Positive thinking is a practice, one that you work with daily and apply regularly. By making it a daily habit you create a positive-thinking mindset that allows you to avoid potentially negative and challenging situations, and helps you resolve dilemmas quickly and easily. With a positive thinking pattern in place you naturally enjoy a better, more rewarding life.

You will attract what you think about regularly, so if you regularly think that life is difficult you will attract situations that will make your life difficult. If you think it's difficult to get money, you will attract situations that make it difficult for you to get money or make poor judgments about money.

Every thought is a seed, If you plant crab apples, don't count on harvesting golden delicious apples. To develop a positive-thinking mindset you need to have positive thoughts, and they should be in your mind constantly. The best way to get started is to change the way you think. So start paying close attention to what you think. Every day you catch yourself thinking, ask yourself – What am I thinking about? Is this thought positive or negative? Does it help me improve my life or does it make my life more difficult?

Most are as happy as they make up their minds to be. Your thoughts and emotions affect all aspects of your life. Learning to be mindful of your —internal dialogue will help you recognize thought patterns and how they may be affecting the way you handle your failures and the situations of daily living. Don't be amazed that many people destroy their own lives with their own tongues. They curse themselves. Remember today you are a result of what you confessed yesterday. If you confessed positive things about yourself, your life is definitely taking a positive direction, but if you confessed negatively, your words have created your world. Learn to form images of what you want in your mind. Live and confess what you want for there is power in your tongue.

> *A man's belly shall be satisfied with the fruit of his mouth; and with the increase of his lips shall he be filled. Death and life are in the power of the tongue and they that love it shall eat the fruit thereof*
> **Proverbs 18:20-21**

The words that we speak are either death or life. We either give ourselves hope or discouragement. Since we are held responsible for every word we speak, we had better listen very carefully to what we are saying, not just to our brethren, but also to ourselves. Jesus said,

> *"But I say unto you, that every idle word that men shall speak, they shall give account thereof in the Day of Judgment. For by thy words thou shalt be justified, and by thy words thou shalt be condemned"*
> **Matthew 12:36-37**

All evil and failure come forth from the heart and proceed out of the mouth.

Jeremiah 17:9 —*The heart is deceitful above all things, and desperately wicked: who can know it?*

Matthew 12:34 "...For out of the abundance of the heart the mouth speaketh"

Matthew 15:18-19 *"But those things which proceed out of the mouth come forth from the heart; and they defile the man. For out of the heart proceed evil thoughts, murders, adulteries, fornications, thefts, false witness, blasphemies"*

When we misuse our tongue we bring disaster to our lives. The Bible continues to say **in James 3:6-11,**

And the tongue is a fire, a world of iniquity: so is the tongue among our members, that it defileth the whole body, and setteth on fire the course of nature; and is set on fire of hell, for every kind of beast, and of birds, and of serpents, and of things in the sea, is tamed, and hath been tamed of mankind: But the tongue can no man tame; it is an unruly evil, full of deadly poison. Therewith bless we God, even the Father; and therewith curse we men, which are made after the similitude of God. Out of the same mouth proceedeth blessing and cursing. My brethren, these things ought not so to be. Doth a fountain send forth at the same place sweet water and bitter?

It is placed upon the ability of your mind to either bless yourself or curse yourself as well as others. The sorrows you are going through may not be coming from where you are laying your blame, but rather from yourself.

Change what you think and you shall be able to change what you are. You are not a failure; you are more than a victor. The more clear and definite you make your mental picture of the success you want, the more you dwell upon it, bringing out all its delightful details, the stronger your desire will be. And the stronger your desire, the easier it will be to hold your mind fixed upon the picture of your success. Failure will go under when you think and meditate success.

Something more is necessary in positive thinking than merely seeing the picture of success clearly. If that is all you do, you are only a dreamer, and will have little or no power for accomplishment. Behind your clear vision must be a positive confession with your tongue, the purpose to realize it and bring it out in tangible expression. And behind this purpose must be an invisible and unwavering faith that what you want is already yours, that it is at hand, and you have only to take possession of it.

Whatever the mind of man can conceive and believe, it can achieve. This is caused by having a Positive Mental Attitude (PMA). Everyone sees life as he or she is. Some people look at the world and see a place of sorrow while others look at the same world and see a place of opportunities. One man will look at the stones on his land and see obstacles to his farm while another will look at the same stones and see an added value of free building materials.

We see life as we are not as it is. Life is how you see it - positive or negative, success or failure, that's what it is. For us to succeed, we must have a paradigm shift as Stephen Covey puts it. A paradigm from the Greek language means model, theory, assumption, perception or frame of. You need a shift in your perception to life if you want to succeed.

Many times we don't need a change of environment but a change of mindset. Failure does not start from without but from within. Where you were when you failed, others succeeded right there. So the geographical location may not be the problem, we are mostly the problem.

Whatever thing you want to achieve is determined by your state of mind. Make a mental shift and see yourself grow. You should be able to think big no matter where you are. Live in the new house, mentally, until it takes form around you physically. In the mental realm, enter at once into full enjoyment of the things you want.

Dwell upon your mental picture of what you want until it is clear and distinct, and then take the mental attitude of ownership towards everything in your mental picture. Take possession of it, in mind, in the full faith that it is actually yours and confess it. Hold to this mental ownership. Do not waiver for an instant in the faith that it is real and yours.

A POSITIVE ATTITUDE

Success depends more on attitude. Winston Churchil said attitude is a little thing that makes a big difference. Attitude is a mental position, relative to a way of thinking or being; a leaning towards that which you believe. A positive attitude is, therefore, the inclination to generally being in an optimistic, hopeful state of mind. Your attitude determines your altitude.

Positive attitude helps you to cope more easily with your failures and the daily affairs of life. It brings optimism into your life, and makes it easier to avoid worry and negative thinking. If you adopt it as a way of life, it will bring constructive changes into your life, and make you happier, brighter and more successful. With a positive attitude you see the bright side of life, become optimistic and expect the best to happen.

A positive attitude leads to success and can change your whole life. If you look at the bright side of life, your whole life becomes filled with light. This light affects not only you and the way you look at the world, but also your whole environment and the people around you.

Negative attitude has killed many big dreams. People have buried their dreams in the graves of self-pity and low self-esteem. Some people because of a negative word from a friend have totally given up on life never to rise up again.

It is said there are four factors of success - information, intelligence, skill, and attitude, but the greatest of all is attitude. For you to succeed, you need a strong positive attitude towards yourself, your dreams, and life. The poor and the rich are as a result of attitude not chances. Though *time and chances happen to them all* (see Ecclesiastes 7:11), what you do when the chances and the time come makes the whole big difference.

> *Rich and poor have this in common the Lord is the maker of them all* **Proverbs 22:2**

If God made men equal where does the difference come from if not from attitude? Even if you have a poor family background, there is always a chance in life for you to rise above your family failures and change the story. That chance comes in form of an opportunity, some people see it and change while others see it and remain the same.

A positive attitude is developed. In life you must learn to give a deaf ear to every negative voice and see yourself successful.

The Philippians had developed a negative attitude towards themselves due to persecutions and anxiety. Some people had discouraged them and they were not positive towards life. Paul wrote a letter to them trying to change their attitude towards life. He begins by telling them to rejoice always. Happiness strengthens the soul and is like healing to the bones, he also tells them to avoid anxiety which brings negative attitude, and then he says

> *Finally brethren whatever is true, whatever is noble, whatever is right, whatever if pure, whatever is lovely, whatever is admirable, if anything is excellent or praise worthy think about such things.* **Philippians 4:8**

Attitude is a battle of the mind and you have to feed your mind with the right stuff.

The Conscious and Subconscious mind

A person's mind is made of two modes; conscious and subconscious. The conscious mind is fed information by the soul, while the subconscious mind is fed information by the eyes, ears, and the other senses of the body. The conscious mind has the faculty of discrimination, carrying with it the responsibility of choice. It has the power of reasoning- whether inductive, deductive, analytical or syllogistic .It can sometimes control the subconscious mind. The conscious mind is the reasoning will. It is responsible for reversing will in your life.

The subconscious mind brings ease and perfection. It is enormous, it guides us to the right things, it warns us, it controls the vital processes in our bodies, it is the seat of memory and it is the distinctive desire. The subconscious mind is the store house of memory. It harbor the wonderful thought messengers which work unhampered by time or space. It is the fountain of practical initiative and constructive force of life. It is the seat of habit. It is the source of ideas of aspiration of imagination and it is the channel through which we recognize our divine source and as we recognize this divinity we come into understanding of the source of power which is God Almighty.

For you to develop a positive attitude, you must rely on the subconscious more than the conscious. The food of the conscious is the physical world while the food of the subconscious is faith which comes from the word of God and other positive information.

Feed your mind with positive information daily. Read testimonies of people who succeeded in what you are doing or planning to do and you will be edifying yourself. This is simply a lift to rise above being a failure to an all day success.

Stay Out of Your Own Way

The first and best victory is to conquer yourself. In my entire life, I have never met a man who has given me as much trouble as myself. We often blame people, situations or environments for our failures, but many times we need a change of ourselves rather than change of the environment.

No one is able to hold you back but yourself; only you can stand in your way. There is an internal critic in you whom you need to silence if you will rise above failure.

If you want to move your greatest obstacle, realize that the first and greatest obstacle is yourself and that the time to act is now.

After my first Visa application to the United Kingdom, I was denied. I since then developed a negative attitude and thought I would never be granted a Visa again. I thought I was going to suffer the same shame even I tried it again.

When I organized a Kenyan Diaspora Investment conference in United Kingdom, I had no option but to apply for a Visa. I knew I had to develop a positive attitude. When I changed my attitude, I got my six months Visa without problems. Positive attitude has a way of opening its own door to success. It brings about confidence, which is a strong weapon against failure. You can't claim to have faith while you have a negative attitude

The mountains and problems you see, most of them exist in your imagination. I have since then realised that; there are two forces that wedge war against each other in our minds. One says, you can't while the other says, With God, you can. The truth is, with God all things are possible.

> **Luke 27:18** (KJV) ....*The things which are impossible with men are possible with God.*

Never build a case against yourself or become an enemy of your own. What we are, good or bad, is what we have thought and believed. If you want to succeed in life, stay out of your own way

If we can tell ourselves that we can make it and then we believe it, then there is no task too big for us. You must begin to think of yourself as becoming the person you want to be.

It is easier to do all the things you should do than spend the rest of your life wishing you had.

Everybody else sees you as a hero, though you see yourself a failure. Have you ever met someone and he/she gives you a big title, or a compliment? Many times we answer back —it's nothing! Or —am flattered these replies we give are mostly an indication that what they think of us is not what we think of ourselves. According to your mind, you are nothing.

You can't consistently perform in a manner that is inconsistent with the way you see yourself, says Zig Ziglar.

The spies who went to spy the Promised Land came back with different reports. Their report clearly shows that victory and failure depend on the heart condition more than the situation.

The Bible says,

> *They came back to Moses and Aaron and the whole Israelite community at Kadesh in the Desert of Paran. There they reported to them and to the whole assembly and showed them the fruit of the land. They gave Moses this account: —We went into the land to which you sent us, and it does flow with milk and honey! Here is its fruit. But the people who live there are powerful and the cities are fortified and very large. We even saw descendants of Anak there. The Amalekite live in the Negev; the Hittites, Jebusites and Amorites live in the hill country; and the Canaanites live near the sea and along the Jordan. Then Caleb silenced the people before Moses and said, —We should go up and take*

possession of the land, for we can certainly do it. But the men who had gone up with him said, —We can't attack those people; they are stronger than we are.And they spread among the Israelites a bad report about the land they had explored. They said, —The land we explored devours those living in it. All the people we saw there are of great size. We saw the Nephilim there (the descendants of Anak come from the Nephilim). We seemed like grasshoppers in our own eyes, and we looked the same to them.

Numbers 13:26-33

While Joshua and Caleb saw the goodness of the land and the possibilities of taking it, the other ten spies who had equal opportunities and evidence as these two, had a different negative story to tell. Nobody called them grasshoppers but themselves, nobody told them they were not able to overcome but their minds. And because they saw themselves as grasshoppers in their own eyes, they looked the same to them. The truth is; even the sons of Anak feared the Israelites due to the report that they had concerning the victories that God had given them throughout their journey from Egypt.

We need more of Calebs today than the other ten. Have you ever met a snake in a bush or somewhere it is not caged? Both of you are afraid of each other. As you run from it fearing, the snake takes the opposite direction fearing you too. This means that what you fear, fears you as well.

Whether you are eleven, forty, or sixty years old, your attitude is still under construction. It's never too late for a person to change his attitude. Just develop a positive attitude. See yourself as able and well gifted for the success you want.

Chapter Six

Rise Above Fear

So do not fear for I am with you, do not be dismayed for I am your God'

Rise Above Fear

So do not fear for I am with you; do not be dismayed for I am your God,
Isaiah 41:10

—For I am the Lord, your God, who takes hold of your right hand and says to you, Do not fear, I will help you.
Isaiah 41:13

Fear is a very strong weapon that Satan uses to kill our visions and dreams. This is one thing that the Bible warns against the devil. The devil knows that if he succeeds in creating fear in you then you will become a useless person who can't change anything in life. The opposite of fear is faith. Faith depends on God's word which is eternal.

Fear is formed in the conscious mind while faith is formed in the subconscious mind. You can never overcome fear unless you learn how to trust in God and have faith in him alone. David said,

When I am afraid, I will trust in you. In God, whose word I praise, in God I trust; I will not be afraid. What can mortal man do to me? **Psalm 56:3-4**

We become afraid when we stop trusting in God. Solomon, the wisest man and a great king, knew he could not make it in his leadership if this he didn't trust in God. He advised,

> *Trust in the LORD with all thine heart; and lean not unto thine own understanding. In all thy ways acknowledge him, and he shall direct thy paths.*
> **Proverbs 3:5-6** (King James Version)

Some fears that hinder our success are:

i. Fear of unseen danger (terror) or destruction

Most people are afraid of losing their jobs and their ability to provide for their families. This feeling of vulnerability often fosters a resignation to riskless living and to co-dependency with others at work and at home. Unseen dangers are formed in the mind of people through imaginations. Some people become afraid of starting a business because they are afraid of failing to succeed. Others are afraid of employing people to run their business because they are afraid of them stealing or mismanaging the business. All these are formulated fears in our minds which hinder us to succeed. It is a scheme of the devil.

You can never succeed if you don't deal with these fears. Remember life has no rehearsal. Live life and learn from it. Don't shy away from your vision because of what you hear or see. You must learn to be a risk taker.

People who succeed in life are risk takers. David said in Psalm 91:5-10 *You will not fear the terror of night nor the arrow that flies by day nor the pestilence that stalks in darkness nor the plague that destroys at midday.*

A thousand may fall at your side, ten thousand at your right hand but it will not come near you.... If you make the Most High your dwelling even the Lord who is my refuge then no harm will befall you, no disaster will come near your tent.

Though you might have seen other people fail in what you want to do, the Bible says even if they fall a thousand on your left side and ten thousand on your right hand, but you shall never be a victim of the same. You shall only observe them fail, but not you, for you have made God your refuge (you trust in him). You will have nothing to fear, terror will be far removed from you. It will not come near you.

> *In righteousness you will be established. Tyranny (terror/ oppression) will be far from you. You will have nothing to fear*
> **Isaiah 54:14**

ii. Fear of adversaries

This is the fear of opponents or our enemies. We all have enemies, either in our businesses, ministry, jobs, families or whatever we do. Sometimes they may be so intimidating like Goliath and David, but we have to be positive towards our victory.

If you are in business, your opponent may stock his shop double size yours and make many advances than you. All this is to intimidate you and to create fear so that you can give up and leave them to monopolise by themselves. Sometimes they may use words that make you feel like you are nothing before them. The devil wants to create a grasshopper mentality in you that was with the ten spies sent by Moses to spy the Promised Land (see Numbers 13).

David didn't allow Goliath to create fear in him. He knew how to fight fear by speaking positive to himself and having a positive attitude. He also had a different perception from the other fighters.

What the Israelite war men saw as a giant to run away from, David saw it as 'a too big a giant to miss'.

As I said before; 'life is how you see it'. If David could have allowed Goliath to intimidate him, he could never have won the battle. When our opponents speak negative and intimidating words against us, we should have word to counter them. David had words to counter intimidating words of fear right from his brothers, Saul and then from Goliath.

—*And when the Philistine looked about, and saw David, he disdained him: for he was but a youth, and ruddy, and of a fair countenance. And the Philistine said unto David, Am I a dog that thou comest to me with staves? And the Philistine cursed David by his Gods. And the Philistine said to David, Come to me, and I will give thy flesh unto the fowls of the air, and to the beasts of the field. Then said David to the Philistine, Thou comest to me with a sword, and with a spear, and with a shield: but I come to thee in the name of the LORD of hosts, the God of the armies of Israel, whom thou hast defied. This day will the LORD deliver thee into mine hand; and I will smite thee, and take thine head from thee; and I will give the carcasses of the host of the Philistines this day unto the fowls of the air, and to the wild beasts of the earth; that all the earth may know that there is a God in Israel. And all this assembly shall know that the LORD saveth not with*

sword and spear: for the battle is the LORD's and he will give you into our hands.
1 Samuel 17:42-47 (King James Version)

Likewise, when the twelve spies went to spy the Promised Land, they returned ten of them with a negative report. They feared what they saw and heard. They saw them as grasshoppers compared to the people of that land. Nobody called them grasshoppers, but that's the image they created in their minds and so did they become. That's why I said; 'you can't be better than what you think'.

Remember the spies; they gave Moses this account -

—*We went into the land to which you sent us, and it does flow with milk and honey. Here are its fruits. But the people who live there are powerful and the cities are fortified and very large, We even saw descendants of Anak there....the land we spied devours those living in it...All the people we saw there are of great size...We seemed like grasshoppers in our own eyes, and we looked the same to them*
Numbers 13:27-33

Fear is an image we create in our minds. Your opponents may seem greater and intimidating, but remember that's according to you. How can a land devour its inhabitants and they are still alive? Those are voices of cowards. Don't allow your negative imaginations to kill your dream.

I said that what you fear, fears you too. The people, whom the spies feared, were the ones who had more fear. If God is with you, nothing is too difficult for you.

The Caleb spirit

—Then Caleb silenced the people before Moses and said, — We should go up and take possession of the land, for we can certainly do it.
Numbers 13:30

If you want to succeed, always intimidate what intimidates you and never allow it to intimidate you. Always remember you have a big God. Bigger and mightier than your problems or enemies is our God. You may not be able to overcome them, but then you are not alone, God is with you. Stop showing God your big problems and start showing your problems your God. Success or Failure is brought by the resolutions you make about yourself.

Be strong in the Lord and in his Mighty Power
Ephesians 6:10

Don't do anything in your own strength; always rely on God's power. When David was challenged by Goliath, he did not allow his conscious mind to show him how big Goliath was but he used his subconscious mind to build his faith in God to see Goliath like a small boy. I wonder who the Giant was. David saw his big God standing against a mortal uncircumcised Goliath. It is not about your size, education or background, but it is about the Mighty God you have who qualifies you when everybody around you has been disqualified. Fear not, for the battle belongs to the Lord.

The Lord is my light and my salvation whom shall I fear? The Lord is the stronghold of my life – of whom shall I be afraid, when evil men advance against me to devour my flesh, when my enemies and my foes attack me they will stumble and fall.
Psalm 27:1-2

Even if your opponents use magic and witchcraft to succeed, do not envy them. They may seem to succeed fast than you, They may even seem to overtake you. Stop complaining and murmuring rather learn from David who said, —*Some trust in chariots and some in horses, but we trust in the name of the Lord our God. They are brought to their knees and fall but we rise up and stand firm* **Psalm 20:7- 8**

Sometimes David feared due to the success of his enemies but he made affirmations of faith before God which were to counter the fearful thoughts.

For I (David) envied the arrogant when I saw the prosperity of the wicked. They have no struggles; their bodies are healthy and strong. They are free from the burdens common to man; they are not plagued from human ills. Therefore, pride is their necklace, they clothe themselves with violence ... They scoff, and speak with malice; in their arrogance they threaten oppression... this is what the wicked are like, always carefree. They increase in wealth.... (David thought) Surely in vain have I kept my heart pure, in vain have I washed my hands in innocence... When I tried to understand all this, it was oppressive to me, till I entered the sanctuary of God, then I understood their final destiny. Surely you (God) place them on slippery ground; you cast them down to ruin,

how suddenly they are destroyed, completely swept away by terrors! As a dream when one awakes, so when you arise, O Lord, you will despise them as fantasies
Psalm 73:3-20

iii. Fear of shame

Many people fear starting off small. They think of what people will say. Unless you overcome this fear, you may never start anything. Everything starts like a mustard seed, small and unrecognized. But if you keep doing it, your shame shall be turned into fame.

Those who saw Nehemiah beginning the walls of Jerusalem thought he was crazy. They mocked to shame him so that he could stop building it.

You need to assume the negative words that inflict fear to you from people.

—Tobias the Ammonite who was at his side said, —What they are building-if even a fox climbed up on it, he would break down their wall of stones.
Nehemiah 4:3

If you fear starting small because some people may mock you, then you need to borrow a leaf from Nehemiah. You may start small, but the dream is big. When you have a dream, you don't look at where you are standing, but where you are heading to. Even if you start by distributing eggs with a bicycle, see it as your mustard seed, God shall establish you in righteousness, and grow your business.

—Hear me, you who know what is right. You people who have my law in your hearts. Do not fear its reproach of men, or be terrified by their insults. For the moth will eat them up like a garment; the worm will devour them like wool...
Isaiah 51:7

Say no to fear of any kind and you shall rise above failure. Be strong and courageous like Joshua. Face your fears and overcome them. Join David to say,

Therefore we will not fear, though the earth gives way, and the mountains fall into their heart of the sea, though its waters roar and foam and the mountains quake with their surging.
Psalm 46:2-3

For the Lord urges us saying;

—... Fear not, for I have redeemed you; I have summoned you by name. You are mine, when you pass through the waters I will be with you. When you pass through the rivers, they will not sweep over you, when you walk through the fire you will not be burned, the flames will not set you ablaze.
Isaiah 43:1- 2

We have the spirit of God. He lives in us and fights for us.

For God did not give the spirit of fear: but of power and of love and of a sound mind.
II Timothy 1:7

Fear can also be caused by painful memories of traumatic experiences, guilt of real or imagined things, generational curses, attacks from the enemy, misunderstandings about God, and/or occult involvement.

To overcome fear:

1. Imagine yourself meeting your goals no matter what people say, or the appearance of conditions. Don't allow anything or anyone to intimidate you; whether time, people or money.
2. Block out negative remarks by others. Whatever people say, count it as there opinion, but listen to what God is saying. It is God who gives us the power to overcome.
3. Avoid negative self-talk. Always be positive to yourself.
4. Keep yourself around positive-minded people. Surround yourself with makers of destiny.
5. Always prepare before action. When you have spent time preparing, you don't get weighed down by fears created by people. You are rather sure of yourself, and know that God has spoken to you. Paul said he counted his present suffering as nothing compared to the glory set ahead of him, and so should you.
6. Choose to trust in God. When you feel like you are afraid of anything, lift your eyes to Jesus to strengthen you. Remember to trust in the Lord in all that you do. Remember,

—...When the enemy shall come in like a flood, the Spirit of the LORD shall lift up a standard against him.
Isaiah 59: 19

7. Engraft God's Word into your soul. The word of God brings light to your life that will help you see your direction. The Lord speaks through his word and builds confidence in us, and fear has no place where the word of God has taken root.

Your word is a lamp to my feet
Psalm 119:105

8. Use positive confessions of faith; acknowledge God's presence in your life. And Close the door to the enemy.

Always remember faith ends where fear begins and fear ends where faith begins. Fear holds you back from flexing your risk muscle. Fear is believing your doubt and doubting your believe. Fear is a dark room where negatives are developed.

Chapter Seven

Embrace Makers of Destiny

He who walks with the wise becomes wise

Makers of Destiny

He who walks with the wise becomes wise
Proverbs 13:20

You need the assistance of people around you to help you get to succeed. Everybody needs somebody to walk with in any discipline of life. You need at least someone to share things with or to encourage you.

—Two are better than one, because they have a good reward for their labour; For if one falls, the one will lift up his fellow but woe to him that is alone when he falleth; for he hath not another to help him up. **Ecclesiastes 4:9-10** (King James Version)

The kind of people you hang around with produce you. You become what your friends are. There are those people you need and there are others you don't need. You need people who, after you have been with them, you find yourself less critical, fuller of faith and with a vision for the future.

It is obvious that if I am going east, I need somebody going in my direction to walk with or someone who has been to where I am going to direct me. Otherwise someone going in the opposite direction can never be my companion, neither can I ask them for direction. Be careful whom you ask for advice or whom you share your vision with. Some people add value to your life while others don't. If you have a friend who does not add any value to your life you need to get rid of them as soon as possible. Some people only drag us behind and pull us down from achieving our dreams.

There are two categories of people you need in order to succeed:

1. People whom you share dreams and ideas with; people you are in the same level with or almost at the same level. You are likely joined together by similar circumstances. An example of this kind of relationship is that of the four lepers in II Kings 7:3-13. They found themselves together because they had something in common. The challenges they went through at that time brought them together to encourage each other and they became friends. You need these kinds of people because they know what you are going through, and they feel your pain. They are best suited for prayer partners. A little caution though; you don't need many of them in order to avoid spending much time talking about where you are instead of where you are heading to.

2. The second category of people are those that are ahead of you in what you are doing or planning to do. They have more experience and expertise in what you hope to be your area of operation. They can mentor you and/ or advice you. For one to succeed in life you need these kinds of people around you. Listen to their advice and take heed of what they tell you.

Iron sharpens iron
Proverbs 27:17

Make sure you only keep positive-minded people around you. If you surround yourself with negative-minded people you will become negative-minded too. Always avoid critics, though sometimes critics are good because they challenge you to do things right, and that criticism is a part of your supernatural promotion. Criticism is the language of the devil. He uses criticism to tear you down. People who always criticize what you are doing are the wrong company to keep.

Always remember those who criticize you are behind you. It is jealous and malice that cause such people to talk about you.

They are simply agents of the devil; Satan always attacks those who can hurt him most. God works from inside out while Satan works from outside in.

The fear of criticism is a kiss of death in the courtship of achievement. If someone belittles you, he is only trying to cut you down to his size. Small minds are the ones that criticize great ideas. Do not fear critics because If you are afraid of criticism, you will die doing nothing. A successful man is one who can lay a firm foundation with the stones that others throw at him. That is why God told Jeremiah in **1:17.**

....Do not be terrified by them, or I will terrify you before them.

Your association may change as you grow up towards success. Some of your friends will be left behind while others may fight against you. Someone said, —Friends who don't help you climb, will want you to crawl. Your friends will either stretch your vision or choke your dream. Don't let mediocre people create your world, for when they do, they will always make it too small. In your highway to success you need people who have succeeded to show you the way. They must have values that match yours.

Plans fail for lack of counsel, but with many advices they succeed **Proverbs 15:22**

Every king needs a king-maker as every destiny needs a destiny-maker. Makers of destiny are like a reference to your journey. When you have one you feel safe. When you are stuck, or meet a challenging situation, he/she can help rise up from your failure. Mentors through their knowledge and experience sharpen your tools of work and you will use less energy.

If the axe is dull and its edge unsharpened, more strength is needed but skill will bring success.
Ecclesiastes 10:10

For you to have skills which bring success, you need another skilled person to sharpen your edges. When God sets you towards your destiny, He brings people or someone into your life. God brought Prophet Samuel to King David, and even after Samuel died, Prophet Nathan appeared. Respect those whom God has connected you to help you. God shows His care and concern to His people through other people. Esther needed Mordecai to become a queen.

Be careful when choosing your mentor. Don't just follow anybody. Some people look like they are going somewhere yet they are going nowhere. If you are born again, you must choose a mentor of the same faith as yours. If you a want a mentor for ministry, he should be of the same spirit with you, and experienced in the gifts and the office of ministry you are operating in (calling). Different offices of ministry have different ways of doing things.

Be careful where you enquire directions from on your journey to success. Fortify your life with the right people. Be careful about whoever is creating your world. Never receive counsel from unproductive people. Never discuss your problems with someone incapable of contributing to the solution.

'Launch to the deep' Luke 5:4

Do not let your mentors or friends limit you. A teacher brings up a student who becomes greater than him. You should aim higher than your mentors. 'We all live under the same sky, but we don't all have the same horizon.' To expand your horizons, you must be able to see the greater potential that is within you. Always look at the bigger picture. Don't be afraid to take a bigger step than your mentor or others around or ahead of you. Always aim for the sun for you to land at the moon. You are more than what people say you are. Only God can define your limits. The sky is not the limit. Stretch further than you are. The road to success has no finishing line. We all live under the same sky, but we don't all have the same horizon.

There are 4 kinds of people when it comes to relationships:

1) Some people add something to life (we enjoy them).
2) Some people subtract something from life (we tolerate them).
3) Some people multiply something in life (we value them).
4) Some people divide something in life (we avoid them).

Think about these and classify the people around you.

Chapter Eight

Be Diligent & Enthusiastic

Whatever your hands find to do, do it with all your might

Diligence & Enthusiasm

Diligence

D iligence is a zealous and careful nature in one's actions and work, exemplified by a decisive work ethic, budgeting of one's time, monitoring one's own activities to guard against laziness, and putting forth full concentration in one's work.

Martin Luther King once said, —If a man is called to be a street sweeper he should sweep the street even as Michelangelo painted, or Beethoven wrote music, or Shakespeare wrote poetry. He should sweep the street so well that all the host of heaven and earth will say, 'Here lived a great street sweeper who did his job well.

Whatever your hand finds to do, do it with all your might...
Ecclesiastes 9:10

The word 'might' also means 'diligence'. We may have good plans, good ideas, great visions, and ambitions, yet if we don't apply diligence in what we are doing, we may get little or no result of the same. Someone else will do the same things, in the same geographical location and receive successful results. Your diligence in today's work should not be determined by yesterday results. Do what your hands have found to do today with all your might.

Diligence also means persistent effort or work. To be diligent is to be steady in application, to be industrious and attentive to duties. It comes from the word 'dilly' which means remarkable or a successful person.

You cannot act where you are not, you cannot act where you have been, and you cannot act where you are going to be, You can act only where you are in other words your effort is not needed where you are not but where you are now. Your diligence in what you are doing now will produce where you will be tomorrow. There are benefits of diligence according to the Holy Bible:

i. Diligence brings wealth

Lazy hands make a man poor, but diligent hands bring wealth.
Proverbs 10:4

It is obvious that even if a man is surrounded by great opportunities, as long as he is lazy, he will never succeed, while a man of diligence will succeed at any given opportunity. Poverty is an opinion. You can choose to be rich or to be poor. The fact that your parents were poor or that you are from a poor background does not mean you should remain and die poor. A poor man has equal chances in his life just as the rich man. It all depends on what you do with the chances. A rich man sees opportunities and goes for them, while a poor man sits on his opportunities waiting for conditions around him to be favorable.

The race is not for the swift or the battle for the strong nor does food come to the wise, or wealth to the brilliant, or favour to the learned but time and chance happen to them all. **Ecclesiastes 9:11**

A life of success is based on opportunities. You can never succeed if you don't discover opportunities in life. The poor see opportunities but they don't go for them. They sit and wait for life to come on a silver platter. If you don't dig the ground you will never get gold. The poor blame the rich for what they have, instead of finding out what the rich do that they do not do. Many opportunities come once in life. If you misuse them or you don't maximise the opportunity, you will live to regret. Those who became successful or made a difference in their generation are simple people who maximised their opportunities. Mordecai, a gate man, realised an opportunity to become the king's in-law and change his life for better. He grabbed the opportunity and gave Esther for a wife to King Xerxes. Years later Esther saved the life of her Uncle Mordecai and all the Jews when Haman the enemy of the Jews plotted against them. Not only that; Mordecai moved from being a gate man to sitting in the palace after Esther saved him from the hands of Haman (see Esther 1, 2, 3).

One maximised opportunity changed Mordecai's life and that of all the Jews. Think of what could have happened if Mordecai could have assumed the opportunity and thought of himself as a gate keeper who had no chance to change his life.

There are certain laws which govern the process of acquiring riches; once these laws are learnt and obeyed by any person, one will get rich. Wealth is as a result of doing things in a certain way. Whether on purpose or accidentally, if one does things this way, they get rich while those who don't do things in this certain way, no matter how hard they work, or how able they are, they remain poor.

Getting rich is not a matter of environment, for if it were, all the people in a certain neighborhood would become wealthy; the people in a certain city would be rich while those of another would all be poor. But everywhere we see the rich and poor living side by side, in the same environment and often engaged in the same vocation. Neither do the rich get rich because they posses talents and abilities that other men have not, but simply because they happen to do things in a certain way.

Among those things that they do in a certain way is diligence. This is not only working hard but also working smart. Bill Gates when asked about his secret of wealth said, —The people you desire to be like don't do things the same as you do, don't sleep as you sleep... John Wesley who wrote over six thousand hymns said, —At seventy I have successfully walked the journey of faith, waking up at 4 am daily. Diligence is a sacrifice and commitment; it is a discipline of the highest order. It is a journey of denying yourself some comfort in order to achieve your goals.

ii. Diligent hands rule

Diligent hands will rule, but laziness ends in slavery labour
Proverbs 12:24

Those employed work hard, long hours with less pay to make others rich. You need to understand that those who have employed you are human like you. If you can follow your dream and apply diligence, then you will one day rule as well. When I learnt this, I took every company that I worked in as my training ground. I learnt what my boss did and how they did things, because I knew that soon I would be running my own company.

To rule means both being ahead and also having people under you. It also means being dominant. With diligence you will dominate (have dominion) in what you do. This is success. God through Adam mandated us to —*have dominion over.* We choose to rule or to be ruled; it is all in your hands.

iii. Diligence will make you dine with kings.

Seest thou a man diligent in his business? He shall stand before Kings: he shall not stand before mean men.
Proverbs 22:29 (King James Version)

Hard work brings forth success, and when you succeed, you will brush shoulders with great men. It may not necessarily be presidents or kings, but you begin to dine with meaningful people in the society. This opens new doors and new opportunities. Once you rise to this level, it is not easy for you to come down again; you begin to operate in levels of continued success.

iv. Diligence will satisfy your desires

The soul of the sluggard desireth, and hath nothing: but the soul of the diligent shall be made fat
Proverbs 13:4 (King James Version)

It is the desire of a poor man that consumes him because what he longs for he cannot attain. His desires lead him to ungodly ways in pursuit of their fulfillment. If you are hardworking, you work for whatever you desire and get it. God blesses the work of your hands, and fulfills the desires of your heart.

Lazy people don't like getting tired; they never desire to pay the price of their labour. As a result, they remain failures in life.

Do not associate with a lazy man for he will spread the disease of laziness to you. Lazy people are the kind that wants to receive miracles that will change their lives without working – the 'microwave blessing' type. But God is not a magician; there is always a price to pay in life in order to succeed.

Lazy people blame everybody for their misfortune. They spend their lives standing at the complaint counter. You must stop living your life as an explanation; live as an exclamation. Any complainer will tell you that success is luck not hard work. But the more you complain the more you will abstain from work. Those who are not aiming at succeeding always see the bad side of situations. Successful people see opportunities even in negative situations.

Some people say they could remove mountains if only someone else would clear the rocks out of their way. They are full of excuses. Men of success don't sit waiting for conditions to be better; they start in diligence and believe things will get better as they move on.

I challenge the sluggard to stop desiring with their mouth. It is one thing to plan; it is another thing to implement the plans. Doing what we want to do is life, and there is no real satisfaction in living if we are compelled to be forever doing something complaining.

If you don't like your job (and that's why you don't work hard), then look for what you are good at and do it diligently. Time is not waiting for you. Everyday you become a day older than yesterday and soon you will be retired. The question is: what have you achieved up to now? It is certain that you can do what you want to do. The desire to do it is proof that you have within you the power which can do it. Go for what you want and do it diligently for profit, satisfaction, and success are in it.

v. A diligent person prices his possession

A hard-working person decides his wages. With hard work you will succeed in what you do, and then you will be able to decide on what to be paid since you prove to be a performer. There are places where some junior employees earn more than their managers due to their diligence. They earn bonuses and commissions that exceed the salary of their seniors. The sky is not the limit; you can fly as high as you dream.

You will be able to price your possession in business when you diligently do it. People will look for you because of your unbeatable services or the packaging of your goods.

> *The lazy man does not roast his game (meat)*
> **Proverbs 12:27**

Unlike the diligent, the lazy man does incomplete jobs and so nobody desires to buy from him or to work with him. We are in a competitive world and to succeed in it we must produce competitive results which come from diligence in work.

Enthusiasm

According to the freedictionary.com, enthusiasm is a Greek word which originally meant inspiration or possession by a divine afflatus (the Latin term translated as "inspiration") or by the presence of God. [from Greek enthousiasmos, from enthousiazein, *to be inspired by a god*, from entheos, *possessed* : en, *in* + theos, *god*]

I therefore define it as a 'strong Godly emotion towards success or victory.' You must continually be visionary and selfmotivated in what you do. Have self-drive towards your vision. Have great eagerness to achieve success in your dreams even when everyone deserts you. Enthusiasm teaches you to remain strong and encouraged in the Lord.

David was deserted by his own soldiers after coming from war. They had found Ziklag burnt down, and their wives and possessions taken away by the Amalekites. The people with David started blaming him for these happenings. They wanted to stone him,

But David encouraged himself in the Lord
1 Samuel 30:6 (King James Version)

The vision is yours and people may not see what you see. Don't expect everyone to understand your dreams. Your employees need to be trained to capture your vision. This is why it is important to write down your goals for every person working with you to understand. These goals will form the reference for all decisions that may be made in your absence by the employees or partners.

Never kill your vision; no matter what happens around you, remain focused and trust worthy. Enthusiasm calls for trust. The word TRUST stands for: **T**ruthful to others, **R**eliability, **U**ncommon effort, **S**ervice, **T**ruthful to self.

T - Truthful to others

You must be totally honest to others, speaking the truth no matter what happens around you. It is the truth that shall set you free. Many people, due to their ungodly desires, lie to get money. This is an evil desire and it's lust. When this evil desire grows you become a con person. You then start using craftiness to acquire wealth. It's dangerous and risky; it will damage your image and/or even make you live without peace and freedom.

I have seen great names being brought to disrepute, being published in newspapers and their image being tarnished permanently. This is not the way to avoid failure or succeed. Fraud doesn't last long. Wealth without character is useless; it is like anointing without character. You can't remain on top without character; your down fall will be great and shameful. Be truthful always so as to be able to stand the test of time.

R - Reliability

For you to succeed in business or in anything you may do, you must be reliable. Be reliable to your customers, to other people, or to your church members as a pastor. Be sure you are able to offer the services you promise. Do not promise what you can't deliver.

Always be on time for appointments. Perfect your services and exercise reliability in your services. Do not keep on apologising to people or your customers for failure of service delivery. People will change to another alternative if they can't rely on your service. Remember you are not the only player in that industry, so do better than others in everything to keep yourself ahead.

U - Uncommon effort

Try to go an extra mile with your clients or your team. Do things that the other players are not doing. Mind your customers, your church followers, or your project team. This makes you successful in places where others have failed. Discover the secret of your work, know the dos and don'ts, the pros and cons, and avoid the pitfalls lest you suffer the consequences others who failed suffered.

There are spirits that rule in every business and every profession. There are principalities and rulers in the heavenlies. We should

> *...destroy their strongholds, cast down imaginations and every thing that exalts itself against the knowledge of God*
> **2 Corinthians 10:4-5**

Always put on the whole armor of the Lord before you go to work. Remember the enemy is at work and we have to overcome him in the name of Jesus Christ. Offer extra services to your clients, be friendly to them, give free samples and extra services than they expect. You earn extra trust from them through these acts.

S - Service

Always offer superb services to your clients. It is similar to offering uncommon effort. Do what your client desires, listen to their complaints and adjust where necessary. Be able to differentiate unnecessary criticism and genuine complaints. Your customer is your employer and it is your duty to satisfy them. Your success is in the hands of your customers. No one can succeed alone; you need people. Treat them well and respect them. They will refer others to you and your clientele base will increase. Even pastors should respect their church members. You are servants to them, not masters. Without followers you are not a pastor. This is the true highway to rising above failure.

Give everyone more in use-value than you take from them in cash-value. Satisfying those whom you serve is the key to your success. In business you will call it customer satisfaction, while in ministry it is full impartation. If you are expecting more than you give, then you are not staying long in your success. A plant produces in proportion to the amount of water it takes. If you deny them services they will deny you results. Greed in life is a suicide mission.

T - Truthful to self

Be truthful to yourself .You are the only one who knows your abilities and weakness. You should do analysis of your Strengths, Weaknesses, Opportunities and Threats (SWOT) on yourself. That is to say you should know your strengths, weaknesses, opportunities, and threats in what you are doing. Being truthful to yourself helps you live a fulfilled and a peaceful life. Don't chew more than you can swallow. Allow yourself to grow gradually and with time you will incline to the heights of success.

Remain focused and avoid doing too many things which make you ineffective. Doing many things hinders you from doing your best. The person who begins too much accomplishes too little, and he that is everywhere is really nowhere. Staying focused helps one avoid failing unnecessarily.

When you don't have a good reason for doing something you have a good reason for not doing it. You can accomplish a lot if you do one thing that you know best how to do, rather than doing many things that you cannot accomplish.

When you remain focused you will become passionate about your dream. Let people know what you stand for; let them identify you by what you do. That's how you make a name for yourself.

Chapter Nine

Practice Giving

Cast your bread upon the waters, for after many days you will find it

Practice Giving

Cast your bread upon the waters, for after many days you will find it. **Ecclesiastes 11:1**

Giving influences your success in life. A giver will never lack anything good from the Lord. Giving can be broken down into various types according to the Bible.

I. Charity

Charity is the love for fellow men, kindness, and affection. When you are charitable, you don't just give for the sake of giving, but it comes from the heart. There is a connection of the act in the heart, when you show the kindness.

We should always begin life by living for others. It is a blessing to give to the needy, for this is the will of God. Many books about success do not highlight charity and other types of giving as an important key to success.

This is a principle that has been observed by many today, including individuals, churches, companies, organizations, and nations. They have in return seen increase because of being open-handed to the needy. If you want to rise above failure in life, observe these things.

Several scriptures have highlighted some rewards of charity:

He who gives to the poor will lack nothing, but he who closes his eyes to them receives many curses. **Proverbs 28:17**

He who is kind to the poor lends to the Lord and he will reward him for what he does **Proverbs 19:17**

Blessed is he who is kind to the needy
Proverbs 14:21

One man gives freely, yet gain even more; another withholds unduly but comes to poverty, A generous man will prosper, he who refreshes others will be refreshed. **Proverbs 11:24-25**

He who oppresses the poor shows contempt for their maker but whoever is kind to the needy honors God. **Proverbs 14:31**

King Solomon, recognized by Jesus as the richest king to ever live on earth, wrote these proverbs out of experience. He knew one of the principles of success in life is to care for the poor and the needy in the society.

The principle of giving works for both believers and nonbelievers. Cornelius was not born again but he practiced the principle and he increased in wealth. God heard his prayers and commanded Peter to go and introduce him to salvation through Christ Jesus.

He and his family were devout and God fearing he gave generously to those in needs and prayed to God regularly ...

the Angel said to him —Your prayers and gift to the poor have come up as memorial offering before God. **Acts 10:2, 4**

The —fear of God in these verses is stated to show that his gift to the poor contributed to making him a God-fearing man. Giving to the poor and needy should not be left for charity organizations only.

You as an individual, company, church, or nation must give to the poor and the needy. On the contrary, however, some employees frustrate the poor, taking advantage of their desperate situation. The Bible warns,

Do not exploit the poor because they are poor and do not crush the needy in court. **Proverbs 22:22**

He who oppresses the poor shows contempt for their maker **Proverbs 14:31a**

If you want God to prosper your business, pay your employees promptly. Pay them the right measure, because they have a maker who is their advocate. Treat all people as important. Don't have two measures; a large one for the rich, and a small one for the poor. You must have accurate and honest weights and measures so that you may live long in the land God is giving you.

—For the Lord your God detests anyone who does these things, anyone who deals dishonestly **Deuteronomy 25:14-16**

If you underpay your employees or delay their payments intentionally while you are able to pay them better or on time, you are oppressing the poor. You cannot live long in your business. Failure is waiting at the door; change and you shall prosper.

The Bible also warns,

> *Masters provide your slaves with what is right and fair, because you know that you also have a master in heaven.* **Colossians 4:1**

Apart from your staff, spare some money or material things and identify some needy people to support, such as those affected by natural disasters like floods and earthquakes. You can also support diseased people and orphans. When you do this you are lending God (see Proverbs 19:17), and God does not stay with people's debt. He will pay you back.

> *—Give and it will be given to you. A good measure, pressed down, shaken together and running over, will be poured into your lap. For with the measure you use, it will be measured to you.* **Luke 6:38**

Always look for opportunities to do good. If you don't have the time to go to the needy, identify an organization which deals with helping the needy and take your donation there. Do it at your own intervals as the Lord enables you.

> *You will be made rich in every way so that you can be generous on every occasion.* **I Corinthians 9:11**

II. Pay Your Tithes

Bring ye all the tithes into the store house, that there maybe meat in my house, prove (test) me now herewith, saith the Lord of hosts, if I will not open you the windows of heaven, and poor you out blessing, that there shall not be room enough to receive it. And I will rebuke the devourer for your sakes, and he shall not destroy the fruits of your grounds, neither shall your vine cast her fruits before the time in the fields, saith the Lord of host. And all nations shall call you blessed: for ye shall be a delightsome land, saith the LORD of hosts
Malachi 3:9-12

The term 'tithe' that is found in scripture (standing for (maser/asar in Hebrew, and dekate/dekavth in Greek) translates into the tenth; thus, the notion that one should give ten percent of one's monies to the church comes from the meaning of these words. The scriptures tell us that God does not want us to do whatever we want or what seems fit to ourselves.

Obviously, that was not working in the first church, just as it does not work today. So God laid out principles for the running of the new country of Israel, that would provide care for the priests and those in charge.

Tithe is one of the offerings that God has instructed us to give faithfully. Tithing is not bondage to law as some wayward preachers have misled people to believe. These are principles of God that will never change. Life is characterised by giving and receiving.

Tithe is 10% of everything that comes to your hand as yours, and not necessarily money. Even material things should be tithed. Tithing faithfully is valuing your assets and tithing of them. Half obedience is total disobedience. Do not be deceived. God is not mocked by the figures you give to the church; He is moved by your faithfulness. If you have 20 million and give a tithe of 100 thousand this may look like a lot of money to men, but God is not a man. He will categorize you in the group of Annania and Saphira who lied to the Spirit of God not to men. God requires 10% of every increase that you receive. We are not donating to God when we tithe; it is a requirement. Failure to tithe is robbing God.

> —Will a man rob God? Yet you rob me, but you ask, —How do we rob you? in your tithes and offering **Malachi 3:8.**

Failure to tithe is robbery to God. It is unfortunate that a thief is a thief but the worst of all thieves is the one who robs God. The judicial courts of this world can bail a worldly thief out, but who will bail you out if God freezes your accounts and arrests you? I have discovered that it is better to owe men than to owe God. A case with God has no advocate. If God files a case against you for robbing Him no one on this earth can save you. Failure to tithe brings a curse:

> —You are under a curse-the whole nation of you. Because you are robbing me, **Malachi 3:9**

Failure to pay your tithe brings a curse on you, on your company, organization, or church. To be cursed by God is the worst thing that can happen to your journey of success. Your dreams will be scattered because God is the one who gives us power to create wealth (see Deuteronomy 8:18). What happens if He curses us? This means He withdraws the power to create wealth. This definitely sends us on the journey of failure and destruction.

Your tithe is your security

—God prevents pests from devouring your crops and the vine. Your fields will not cast the fruit **Malachi 3:11**

The vine is your dream. If the Lord does not protect the vine, it will cast its fruits before harvest time. This happens when you don't pay your tithes. Even after you have succeeded and you are doing well, remember to be faithful up to the end. The enemies of our success will not rest until they see our downfall. But when we remain faithful in paying our tithes, the Lord rebukes the destroyer for us. Through our tithes, our dreams are protected and we sure of success. There will be no unnecessary deductions from our salaries, no exaggerated hospital bills, no unnecessary breakdown of your properties, and no retardation in business.

If you pay your tithe, God prevents the devourer from devouring your harvest. If you don't tithe, the opposite will happen. He will allow pests/destroyers to enter to your vineyard (business) and destroy what you have laboured for. Tithe is like a security officer employed from heaven to guard your blessing. Failure to tithe is to do away with the security and become vulnerable to attacks from Satan the destroyer. Remember,

Unless the Lord build the house its builder labour in vain, unless the Lord watches over the city the watchmen stand guard in vain
Psalms 127:1

Tithing Unlocks Godly Wisdom of Spending

Those who don't tithe, even though they gather a lot, spend almost every coin in paying bills. Hospital bills, disasters, and other calamities take away what they gather. These blessing-eaters strike when you fail to pay your tithes. When you fail to tithe the scripture below is fulfilled.

In vain you rise early and stay up late, toiling for food to eat – for he grants sleep to those he loves **Psalm 127: 2**

III. Sow your seed

When God created the herbs and the trees, He created them in this fashion - *that in them they had the ability to reproduce "after its kind"* (see Genesis 1:11).

From my observation, it has been from the very beginning that a mango seed brings forth a mango tree and eventually produces mangoes, and that is a factual principle. In moral and spiritual matters, the teaching provides the same principle. What we sow we reap.

Seed-sowing has been grossly challenged especially in the Kenyan society for the misuse of this term. The true principle of sowing and reaping still remains despite the misuse. Though there are imposters, people who are calling themselves servants of God but are not, who are out to rob people of their money, the power of a seed in our success remains. While a copy comes, the original will always be easy to identify.

Sowing can be done in many ways but overall the seed you sow is what you reap. If you sow a seed of goodness, you reap goodness, if you sow rebellion, you reap rebellion, if you sow anger, anger shall you reap, if you sow money, you reap money. And the list is endless.

Be not deceived; God is not mocked: for whatsoever a man soweth, that shall he also reap **Galatians 6:7**

Though whatever you sow is what you reap, the quantity matters too. Many people sow two kilograms of seed and expect to harvest a thousand bags. God is not a magician; there are guiding principles that He follows to bless us in justice.

We determine the size of the harvest at the time of sowing. If you sow sparingly, you reap sparingly. If you sow bountifully, you reap bountifully. You hold the key to your abundance. You choose whether to operate in abundance or in scarcity during sowing time.

Remember this: Whoever sows sparingly will also reap sparingly, and whoever sows generously will also reap generously... And God is able to bless you abundantly, so that in all things at all times, having all that you need, you will abound in every good work... You will be enriched in every way so that you can be generous on every occasion, and through us your generosity will result in thanksgiving to God. **II Corinthians 9:6, 8, 11**

The man who gives beyond his tithe will operate in overflow as well. The more one gives, the more one reaps. Giving brings God great pleasure. And He desires for the abundance to us that overflows to he who gives without measure. When Jesus fed the 5000, there was great abundance even after the need was met (see John 6:13). This is the kind of prosperity that God desires for His people. The believer should never be satisfied with living from hand to mouth as if God never intended or desired to prosper you. Abundance cannot be given from a meager existence. Rather, the life that overflows with the blessings of God can give as it has received.

> *Honor the LORD with your wealth, with the first fruits of all your crops; then your barns will be filled to overflowing, and your vats will brim over with new wine.* **Proverbs 3:9-10**

We will always have a harvest when we sow -

> *Let us not become weary of doing good, for at the proper time we will reap a harvest if we do not give up.* **Galatians 6:9**

When you sow, you will always reap! This law is as sure as the rising and going down of the sun. The success of this harvest is not determined by natural laws, but the success is governed by the Lord Himself. If you sow your seed into your church from which you and your family receive spiritual nourishment, you and your family will reap a good harvest every time your pastor preaches the Word and sows good seed into your lives and other people's lives.

Your seed requires time to multiply (Patience)

> *—I tell you the truth, unless a kernel of wheat falls to the ground and dies, it remains only a single seed. But if it dies, it produces many seeds.* **John 12:24**

If you are a farmer, or have ever been to a farm, you don't have to be reminded that both growth and decay take time. The same is true of our spiritual seed. Perhaps this is the reason Paul warned that we shouldn't be deceived. Nothing seems to happen right away.

We may receive immediate benefits when we sow into our local church, but your seed may take time to multiply. While we do the sowing, God does the multiplication, and at the proper time we shall reap if we don't give up; at the appointed time of God...

> ..... *for at the proper time we will reap a harvest if we do not give up* **Galatians 6:9**

There is a season for planting and a season for harvesting. Not all harvest follows immediately. The time element is important. If the seed germinates before its proper time, a harvest can be lost or be small.

> *There is a time for everything and a season for every activity under heaven....a time to plant and a time to uproot (harvest).* **Ecclesiastes 3:1, 2**

Many give as if there will not be a harvest. Some people think God did not note what they planted simply because they have not experienced a harvest. But if we plant a seed, a harvest will come. Sometimes we have to continue planting even when we have not seen the harvest of the first seed.

Consider this -

Sow your seed in the morning and do not be idle in the evening, for you do not know whether morning or evening sowing will succeed, or whether both of them alike will be good. **Ecclesiastes 11:6**

The message here is: if we continue to sow our seed, one or all the seeds will succeed in bringing you harvest. Don't sow the first one and fold your hands saying you shall sow next when you harvest the first one. That is not a Kingdom principle of sowing and reaping. We are responsible for the sowing, and God is responsible for the harvest. We are laborers together with God. God does not produce failures; He is the Lord of the harvest. With these laws God has set in order, we need to sow seed that is going to bring harvest both now and in eternity.

Don't wait for a sign of harvest to sow

While you sow, avoid looking at the conditions around, which is like a farmer who watches at the wind to sow. Farmers plant when it is a dry season. Whoever looks at the clouds to sow, will never reap for he will not sow in time. That is to say, do not wait for a sign of harvest for you to sow. Sowing is solely faith-dependant.

Whoever watches the wind will not plant; whoever looks at the clouds will not reap. **Ecclesiastes 11:4**

We will always reap more than we planted if we don't give up. The law of increased return is what makes farming a workable business enterprise, while sowing to God's Kingdom results in divine harvests and a successful life.

—No eye has seen, no ear has heard, no mind has conceived, what God has prepared for those who love him. **I Corinthians 2:9**

IV. Pay Your Vows

—There (in the house of God) bring... what you have vowed ...: **Deuteronomy 12:6**

A vow is defined as a promise offering that would be kept or given by the individual if God would do something for them.' The Hebrew word is *neder*.

There are times we want God to do something special in our lives, and we vow before Him. Hannah asked God for a son and vowed that she would give the child to God as a Nazarite (to serve in the Lord's temple). When she had weaned him, she took him and her offerings to the temple in Shiloh. The Lord then kept His part of the bargain and the child became a prophet. Hannah wanted a son. It was something she had longed for, for a long time. The bible says,

... and she made a vow saying —O Lord Almighty if you will only look upon your servant's misery and remember me, and not forget your servant but give her a son, then I will give him to the Lord for all the days of his life and no razor will ever be used on his head **I Samuel 1:11**

This is an example of a vow. God honors vows. He granted the need of Hannah and gave her a baby boy. In I Samuel 1:2728 Hannah fulfilled her vow by taking Samuel to the house of God as she had promised. Samuel became a servant in the temple and later a prophet. Later Hannah was blessed with more children. Vows are made in companion with prayers of specifications.

> *Don't be quick to vow, or to vow what you can't fulfill. Better that thou shouldest not vow, than that thou shouldest vow and not pay. Suffer not thy mouth to cause thy flesh to sin; neither say thou before the angel that it was an error; wherefore should God be angry at thy voice, and destroy the work of thine hand.* **Ecclesiastes 5:5-6** (King James Version)

Be careful not to be a victim of being unfaithful by failing to pay your vows. Jephtha vowed to give whatever met him from the war if God granted him victory. God fulfilled his part by giving him the victory he asked for. Jephtha was met by his only daughter, and he had to fulfill his part of vow by killing his only daughter (see Judges 11:29-40).

To vow to God is to enter into a covenant with Him. God is not a man; He is a covenant-keeping God. He will always do His part and He expects you to do your part as you promised. His 'Yes' is a 'Yes' and his 'No' is a 'No'. He challenges us to have the same principles. Vow and fulfill the vow. Follow the terms of the covenant even if they are difficult. As desperate as we seem when we are making the prayer of covenant to God, we should not try playing a hide and seek game with Him when He blesses us. We can't run away from God. Though today you have got what you wanted from God, tomorrow you may need Him for something else. Keep a good relationship with God through obedience.

V. Give Freewill offerings

This was an offering given voluntarily for the work of the Lord. A freewill offering could be given at the pastor's request. Those who were willing would give generously. For example, the Jews who had a willing heart were requested by Moses to bring offerings of precious stones, anointing oil, linen, and other items to build the tabernacle in the wilderness. The Bible says in Exodus 35:21 and 36:3b, 4-6,

> *... and every one who was willing and whose heart moved him came and brought an offering to the Lord for the work on the tent of meeting, for all its service, and for the sacred garments....the people were so willing that they brought the offerings every morning...Their gifts were so abundant that Moses had to ask the people to stop bringing them in*

These are offerings that we give in the church when there are special projects like church construction or purchase of church property. They serve as a sign of our commitment to God. If you love God, you shall serve Him with your possessions. When you make your possessions God's possessions, He will always supply to you enough to meet your needs and serve Him.

> *You will be made rich in every way so that you can be generous on every occasion...***2 Corinthians 9:11**

VI. Give your First fruits

When we receive a harvest (an increase that we didn't have before) from a new job, salary increment, first payment from a new project, or any other source, we should give those first fruits to the Lord. In Exodus 23:16 there was a festival in Israel which was meant to celebrate the harvest; people brought their first fruits to the altar.

—...bring the best of the first fruits. **Exodus 23:19**

When you give do not give grudgingly as though someone is pushing you. Always remember you are the one who needs God's intervention into your life. Giving is part of our worship to God. We give as a way of worship. God owns everything and deserves everything. He is our Father and all that we have, He gave unto us. How then can we deny Him what He generously gave us?

For God loves a cheerful giver. And God is able to make all grace abound to you so that in all things at all times. Having all that you need, you will abound in every good work. **2 Corinthians 9:7b**

VII. Thanksgiving offerings

Do not be anxious about anything but in everything by prayer and petition, with thanksgiving, present your request to God and the peace of God which transcends all understanding will guard your hearts and your minds in Christ Jesus. **Philippians 4:6**

A heart of gratitude is a heart that God honors. Many people become successful through God's blessing but often they take it for granted; they don't bother to go back to God and show gratitude. Gratitude just by a word of mouth is not enough. Never go before the King to say thank you empty-handed. For you to be able to give thanks or to have a grateful heart, you must first believe that there is one Mighty God, from whom all things proceed. Secondly, believe that God gives you everything you desire, and third, relate yourself to Him by a feeling of deep and profound gratitude.

The soul that is always grateful lives in closer touch with God than the one which never looks to Him in thankful acknowledgment. Many people who order their lives rightly in all other ways are kept in poverty by their lack of gratitude to God. Having received a simple success from God, they cut the wires which connect them with Him by failing to make acknowledgment. It is easy to understand that the nearer we live to the source of wealth, the more wealth we shall receive.

> *Enter his gates with thanksgiving and his courts with praise; give thanks to him and praise his name. For his love is good and his love endures forever, his faithfulness continues through generations.* **Psalm 100:4-5**

The more we are grateful and fix our minds on the supreme God when good things come to us, the more good things we will receive, and the more rapidly they will come.

Giving thanks to God will lead your mind out along the ways by which things come, and it will keep you in close harmony with creative thought and prevent you from falling into competitive thought.

Gratitude alone can keep you looking toward the all, and prevent you from falling into the error of thinking of the supply as limited. The mental attitude of gratitude draws the mind into closer touch with the source from which the blessings come.

Ten men were healed from leprosy by Jesus. The ten left but only one came back to say thanks. Jesus wondered where the rest were. This means God expects us to come back to Him and say thank you. Jesus asked,

—*Were not all ten cleansed? Where are the other nine? Was no one found to return and give praise to God except this foreigner? Then he said to him, —Rise up and go; your faith has made you well.* **Luke 17:17**

When we think we have had it all from God and do not go back to give a thanksgiving offering, we are hindered from receiving the better portion of our blessing tomorrow - to be made whole. There is a law of gratitude, and it is absolutely necessary that you should observe it if you are to get the results you seek.

Jesus always took the grateful attitude; He always seemed to be saying, —I thank thee, Father, that thou hearest me. You cannot succeed without gratitude, for it is gratitude that keeps you connected with the source of success. Gratitude consists in getting you more blessings in the future. Without gratitude you cannot long keep from having thoughts of dissatisfaction regarding the way things are. The grateful mind is constantly fixed upon the best. Therefore it tends to become the best. It takes the form or character of the best, and will receive the best.

See that you excel in this grace of giving. **2 Corinthians 8:7**

Chapter Ten

Learn to Invest

God always gives us something to start with

Learn to Invest

God always gives us something to start with. Never say you have nothing; you must learn to start small, to go far. The reason many people have not done anything up to now is because they are waiting for a perfect time when they will have enough. If you wait for perfect conditions you will never get anything done.

Stop waiting for time; time is not waiting for you. The time is now for you to start. Do not allow what you can't do hinder you from doing what you can do.

To invest in your profession does not mean investing money only. Your profession, ministry, or business needs your investment of money, time, and energy. Some people invest so much money in their business but give it too little of their time. This kills the business slowly and you can never succeed this way.

i. Invest Your Time

The most important requirement for what you do is time. Spend time planning, accessing, and evaluating your project. Once you have started something, whether small or big, it needs your attention. Never trust anybody to do what you could do.

Remember you are the vision carrier.

In a case where you are too busy elsewhere, you should get the right people for the job. Set up a system for them to follow. Never let employees run your business with their own ideas. Though they may contribute their views towards the business, always be the controller and be principled.

Research has shown that getting people to employ is easy but getting the right people is not. Your employees can either make or break you. You must lead the way. Train your employees the way you would like your job to be done. Let them know your beliefs and your principles. They must be totally loyal to you and especially the top management. Always speak your mind to your employees.

If you want to have a good team from the start and in future, you must train your first staff members to think like you and see things the way you see them. Make them own the business right from the beginning. Treat them fairly by respecting them and giving them job guarantee. When employees feel insecure, they can ruin your business because they know they may be sacked at any time and so they don't care about the fate of your business.

Time is very precious for any investment, big or small. Give your full attention to your dream like you do a new born baby. Nurse it till it matures to stand on its own two feet.

ii. Invest in Your Energy

Your effort is equally important in your dream especially when it is starting; you must be fully involved in practically all the activities. Sometimes do things yourself. It is not easy for other people to do things the way you would want them done. You must monitor with closeness to avoid tainting the image of your dream before it goes far.

The Art of Success _____

People can only know you by what you have done and not by what you are planning to do.

If you are running a restaurant and it has just started, you need to be there sometimes if not always and see how customer service is being done. Be satisfied with the work of your staff.

Correct where you are not satisfied.

There are other professions that need all your time and energy. You must provide it fully. This is the art of success.

While investing, learn to be focused. Do not scatter your energy investments. Doing too many things always keeps you from doing your best. The person who begins too much accomplishes too little. Someone said, —He who is everywhere is nowhere. There are times to say NO to good ideas. Great people are not known for doing everything but for doing one thing successfully. It is better to do one thing a million times, than doing a million things at one time.

> *Better is a handful with tranquility, than both the hand full with toil and chasing after the wind.* **Ecclesiastes 4:6**

iii. Invest Money

Investing money into your dream is a must. Money answers all things. Whatever you treasure, you will invest your money in it and wherever you invest your money, there your heart will always be.

> —*For where your treasure is there your heart will be also*
> **Matthew 6:21**

Get books that advice on finances and how to run a business. In the Kenyan setup and laws of doing business, there are books like *How to Save Money for Investment, How to Start & Manage Your Own Business*, just to mention but few.

As you invest money into your dream, remember the heavenly investment. Many people forget investing in the Kingdom for their dream's sake. Jesus said,

> —*Do not store up yourself treasures on earth... where moth and rust destroy and where thieves break in and steal. But store up yourself treasures in heaven, where moth and rust do not destroy and where thieves do not break in and steal.*
> **Matthew 6:20**

iv. Invest Into Yourself

You are the first and most important asset to your business. Do not say your business will still run even if you are not there. Though it might be true, things will not be the same. Some people invest so much into their careers and businesses while they starve themselves. Your dream needs you so you should be healthy and fit to provide a good input to it. You should be at your best physically.

Exercise of the body is needed. Apply good health habits and watch the kinds of foods you eat. Remember your life is very important. If you are a pastor or born-again, be wise and be led by the Spirit when you go for fasting. Godly things call for application of wisdom.

You are the first and most important asset to your business. Don't starve yourself because you want to invest. The body functions better when it is well fed and well taken care of. Your family should not suffer hunger and lack basic needs in the name of investment. Discipline is required for you to grow your business, but don't grow your business and die before you eat of its fruits.

Do not be extravagant though. Be disciplined financially. You can visit financial advisors to help you on how to do this. Some jobs are of the kind that will make you meet many people, like sales and marketing. People judge salespeople by their first appearance. People buy from people. Your public image and personality may give you a sale or make you lose it. If you are the director of your business, get yourself some official clothes depending on the type of your business and keep yourself neat. People will then begin to respect your personality even before you speak.

v. Invest in Knowledge

Develop the mastery of your skills through training, learning, seminars, and reading. In whichever industry you are in, there are new developments in doing things better every time. You need to stay up-to-date with the new technology. Adding knowledge in line with what you do is very important; it helps you to stay well informed and you learn how other successful people do their businesses, run their churches, or do their jobs.

If you can duplicate the habits of successful people, you will duplicate their results as well. Invest some money in advancing your education. Many people think you should advance education if you want a new job or if you are employed. Business people should and do go to school too. It is in colleges where you can learn things like financial management, business management, production, and project management among others. As a business owner you need to be ahead of your employees or at least have ideas of what they are doing including accounts.

Knowledge is power they say. Do anything to be ahead of others. In all ways make yourself outstanding in your profession. Do things differently. The difference between the rich and the poor is that there is something the rich do that the poor don't.

The rich do things differently from the poor. One person may have a shop of the same size with another, and after two years one of them has a wholesale depot while the other is still at kiosk level. Why? There is something one did that the other didn't do.

Chapter Eleven

Have Professional Pride

Be Proud of Your Profession

Have Professional Pride

Professional pride simply means being proud of your profession. This is being sure of your value to God and men for who you are and what you do.

Professional pride begins by gratitude. You may not be where you wanted to be but at least you are somewhere. You can never attain success in life unless you have a heart of gratitude to God for what you have. Gratitude, joy, self-esteem, love of your job, and satisfaction define professional pride.

Those who do not have professional pride begin to envy others. If you are comparing yourself with others, your view is distorted. Envy is a tremendous waste of mental energy. Refrain from it for it is the source of most unhappiness and failure. One of the most valuable decisions we can make is not to compare ourselves with other people. Other people's lives and their jobs have nothing to do with what God is doing in your life to make you successful.

You are unique, God created you well-fit for your job. Always adopt your own way and speed of doing things. Know your abilities and limits. Do not imitate others.

When Jacob went to meet his brother Esau together with his flock, Esau wanted Jacob to go at his speed but Jacob told him, in Genesis 33:14,

—Let my Lord (Esau) go ahead of his servants, while I move along slowly at the pace of the droves before me and that of the children until I come to my Lord in Seir.

Professional pride is always taken away by living other people's lifestyles. You are yourself; don't get into competition with anyone. If you work at someone else's speed, you may crash before you get to your destination. Move at your own speed; the destination is one – success – and we shall all get there some day. Allow God to order your steps and, even though you may fall, He will uphold you.

The steps of good man are ordered by the Lord: and he delighted in his way. Though he falls, he shall not be utterly cast down; for the Lord uphold his hand. **Psalm 37:23-24** (King James Version)

When you move at the speed of God, He will deal with your pitfalls; He will lower your mountains and straighten the crooked places for your sake. Allow Him to show you the way and He will open doors before you so that your gates will not be shut.

This is what the LORD says to his anointed, to Cyrus (you), whose right hand I take hold of to subdue nations before him and to strip kings of their armor, to open doors before him so that gates will not be shut: "I will go before you and will level the mountains; I will break down gates of bronze and cut through bars of iron." **Isaiah 45:1- 2**

Professional pride comes from the knowledge that God is with you. It is the peace of God in your heart about your job or business. It is to know that God will make a way where there seems to be no way. It is to have faith in God and to trust in Him.

Happiness and satisfaction are not brought about by the presence of things but by having a dream and trusting in God for its fulfillment.

We seem to lose our professional pride especially when there is a delay of success. You might have done your annual plans and targets but at the end of the period, you fail to hit the targets. Always let the will of God take its course.

To man belong the plans of the heart but from the Lord comes the reply of the tongue....commit to the Lord whatever you do and your plans will succeed....in his heart a man plans his course, but the Lord determines his steps. **Proverbs 16:1, 3, 9**

Do not build a case against yourself if your plans don't go as stipulated. Always know there is a higher authority which determines where you will be and when. This is God. It is of importance that you adopt the pace of God. God is never late. Avoid working under pressure. The art of receiving God's success is patience for there is no time lost in waiting upon the Lord.

All great achievements require time. Avoid falling into the trap which Abraham fell into. The pressure upon Abraham took away his patience. Were it not for his wife's pressure, he would not have taken Hagar and given birth to Ishmael. It required a little more patience for Abraham and Isaac would have been born.

Walking at the pace of God helps or establishes us on the proper foundation. Nothing is permanent unless it builds on God's will and God's word (see Psalm 127:1).

Burn and cool at the same time like a candle, do not burn at both ends.

The road to success runs uphill. So don't expect to break any speed record. Elijah allowed Ahab to run as fast as he could with his chariots and was left on the mountain praying. When Elijah took off, though late, he arrived at Jezreel before Ahab who had started off before him (see I Kings 18:41-45).

Seeking to start your journey with God is more important than starting without Him. When you start running with God, you will overtake even those who went ahead of you, for God's speed is an extraordinary speed. The difference between natural and supernatural is the 'super' while the difference between ordinary and extraordinary is the 'extra'. Our God is extra ordinary and supernatural. Allow Him to take you at His own speed for He knows the road more than you do.

All these are components of professional pride but the most important is self-esteem. The biggest enemy of your progress is not how people see you but how you see yourself. Stop putting blocks on your way. Be positive and know you are called for a higher calling.

As a man thinketh, so is he. **Proverbs 23:7**

You can only become what you see yourself becoming. No one can create your world except you. If you want it small it will be small, and if you want it bigger it will be.

To esteem ourselves high is not pride. Don't live in false humility. Being harmless as doves, as the Bible says, is not an excuse not to try things. Be wise as a serpent too. Break the cocoon of limitations that you have built in your life and wake up in the world of success. For water to find its way to the ocean it has to knock on stones, sweep the debris on the way and create a way for itself. There are frictions on the way to success. Don't allow people to put you down neither should you put yourself down.

High self-esteem is a spiritual weapon that sees giants as boys and boys as giants. Don't look at life through a microscope which amplifies small things and cannot see big things. Look at life through the word of God. You can do what the Bible says you can do. You can be what the Bible says you can be.

When you feed your spirit with the worldly things, the conscious mind that causes discouragement and low self-esteem will be exalted and cause you to fail.

We lie loudest when we lie to ourselves, for you can only perform in the manner that you see yourself. Professional pride will only be developed if you esteem yourself higher for this is the art of success.

Be swift to seize opportunities in life. Be careful not to miss them for many people have missed their opportunities due to low self-esteem. When you classify yourself lowly, you will miss the great opportunities in life.

To know the level of your professional pride, ask yourself the following 10 questions.

i. Do you hesitate when asked what you do for a living?
ii. Do you use a job title that does not really reflect what you do?

iii. Do you want to tell others what you do by yourself?

iv. Would you write a story about what you do positively?

v. Do you define your status by the things you do at work or by the things you have at home? vi. Do you want your kids to do the same job you do in future? Can you recommend it to them?

vi. Do your real friends recommend you as a specialist in your job?

vii. Do you want to explain your job to others?

viii. Are you so proud of your achievements in your job?

ix. If you could choose your profession again, would you take the same a second time?

The above simple questions may help you know if you enjoy what you do or not.

Chapter Twelve

Have the Fear of God

The fear of the Lord is the beginning of knowledge

Have the Fear of God

The fear of the Lord is the beginning of knowledge but fools despise wisdom and discipline **Proverbs 1:7**

I could not talk about the art of success without touching on a core subject. To fear God is to acknowledge Him, which means having a loving reverence for Him. This includes submitting to His Lordship and the command of His word. Many people don't understand what the fear of the Lord means. They think it is being afraid of God. On the contrary, it means acknowledging Him. If we understand what He means we will begin to walk in His abundance of blessings.

The following describes the true meaning of the fear of the Lord.

i. To delight in God

To fear God is to delight in Him and acknowledge that He is truly God. To show Him that He owns us and we cannot do without Him. God loves to show us His good plan for us; to give us our expected end (see Jeremiah 29:11) if we walk in awe of His might.

Delight yourself in the Lord and he will give you the desires of your heart. **Psalm 37:4**

People love quoting the second part of the scripture but they forget the condition. He will give you the desires of your heart if you delight in Him (fear Him).

ii. To acknowledge God

Trust in the Lord with all your heart and lean not your own understanding. In all your ways acknowledge him and he will make your paths straight. **Proverbs 3:5-6**

Our path to success can never be straight if we keep God away from our plans and work. He knows the way to where you are going and He is the best guide to show you the way. If you acknowledge God in what you do, He will surely fight the battles for you. He shall anoint you (empower you) to do the job and you will not struggle.

If we don't acknowledge God and instead we fight our way alone, we shall end up struggling for the rest of our lives and never succeed.

iii. To allow God build your house

Unless the Lord builds the house, its builders labour in vain, unless the Lord watches over the city the watchmen stand guard in vain. In vain you rise early and stay up late toiling for food to eat, for he grants sleep to those he loves. **Psalms 127:1-2**

Your house as per the above verse maybe your job, studies, business, or ministry. If you don't allow God to do it, you are doomed to fail. Even if you toil tirelessly and sleep late, it will never yield anything, for God gives comfort (sleep) to those He loves (those who fear Him).

You are born a success not a failure. Don't look down at yourself nor allow someone else to do so. Worship God as *The* though He is God (see Romans 1:21-22). Learn how to walk in His ways. Love Him with all your heart and strength. If He has done it for others He will do it for you too.

iv. Catch the small foxes

> —*Catch for us the foxes, the little foxes that ruin the vineyards, our vineyards that are in bloom.* **Song of Songs 2:15**

To bloom means flowering. Foxes are small animals found mostly in England; they dig holes in a vineyard. The hole may be distant from the vine tree, but goes all the way to the roots of the vine tree. The little foxes hide and skulk about, doing their best to avoid detection. For the most part, they are nocturnal and operate in the dark. Selah! (Pause and calmly think about that) They also don't root up or destroy the vines completely, but rather stunt their growth; therefore, the vines have no chance of bearing good fruit.

We are the vineyard of the Lord. He has planted vines in us, which are our dreams, gifts, and abilities. Your dreams have already started to bloom (flower) meaning you are about to bear fruit. While your dreams bloom, the small foxes are already destroying them. These are the small sins and mistakes which we easily assume, and never repent and turn away from. The Lord is telling you to catch them (stop them) for they will make you bear no fruit. You will never succeed in anything if you allow those small foxes to destroy the dreams and visions God has planted in your heart.

The little foxes speak of small sins which often go unnoticed by anyone. You say, —Everyone does this, so what's wrong with it? They consume the flowers and impede the fruit. It merits careful attention, in this hour in which we live, to retain the blessing. If the foxes destroy the flowers, we will then have no fruit.

The little foxes are little areas of compromise in our lives, worldly habits and behaviors that are socially acceptable, but which grieve the Holy Spirit. The Bible warns us not to grieve the Holy Spirit by which we were sealed. These things are very easy to rationalize because they are socially acceptable behaviors, even though the Lord dislikes them. They are also easy to hide from the pastor and/or others in the church. We can appear very spiritual and devoted in the church, but have little sins, small worldly influences in our lives. These may be hidden from the eyes of men, but they will still interfere with the success that God desires for us. In the end, there will be little or no fruits of success.

The little foxes are very dangerous because they are sometimes imperceptible. We tell ourselves and everyone else that we are fine spiritually, but there are things we're doing that we know the Lord probably wouldn't like. Then we expect the Lord to give us success and blessings. Our blessings get contaminated; either there will be none at all, or they will be so little that they have no value to us or anyone else.

Geoffrey N. Kilonzo

Little foxes always seem to come around just when we're getting it all together in our dreams. For example, just when everything seems to be going on well, the little fox of 'neglect' shows up; neglect of daily reading of God's Word or neglect of regular prayer time, failure to forgive, failure to tithe, and failure to love.

Chapter Thirteen

Honour Your Spiritual Fathers

Do not rent-a-father, have a legitimate spiritual father

Honour Your Spiritual Fathers

—And he shall turn the heart of the fathers to the children, and the heart of the children to their fathers, lest I come and smite the earth with a curse. **Malachi 4:6**

I dedicate this chapter to all believers - born again Christians, young pastors and ministers of the gospel, gospel artists, church leaders, spiritual fathers, and all those who want to live a life full of God's blessings and divine success. Blessings to you all as you read through this last and greatest chapter in *The Art of Success*.

—Do we still have spiritual sons and spiritual fathers today? This is a question anyone with true revelation about sonship and fatherhood would be asking himself. There is a great deception in the Church today of who a spiritual son or a spiritual father is. Malachi could not have put it clearer than the scripture above because the prophecy is being fully fulfilled today.

Many so-called spiritual fathers are already under a curse while their so-called spiritual sons have inherited the same curse. This curse affects you; from your ministry, to your business, job, marriage, and every sphere of your life. That's why I have decided to write on this topic among the keys of rising above failure.

Who is a Spiritual Father?

The Bible brings a clear image of spiritual fatherhood and sonship on many occasions. Good examples are: Moses and Joshua, Elijah and Elisha, Paul and Timothy, just to mention a few.

As much as there are examples of good sons, there are examples of bad sons and their repercussions too. Examples of these are Gehazi, Demas, and Alexander among others. The use of _sons' and 'fathers' does not eliminate mothers and daughters. God is presented throughout the scriptures as "Father," and is never called "Mother." To dilute this is to distort His image with a very thick veil. "Father" means "life-giver." The father gives the seed, and the mother nurtures the seed. In the scriptures we see the creation as "a" mother. Both Israel and the Church are also referred to in scripture as "mothers." Just as the woman was taken from Adam so that they would have to come together to be the complete image of God, the Lord will be joined perfectly to His bride to give the creation a true reflection of His glory.

Since God calls His corporate body (males and females) both a bride (see Revelation 21:9), and a son (see Romans 4:5-7) it is clear that gender is not the issue here. Being a spiritual father is not related to gender, and a woman can function as a spiritual father just as well as a man (see Galatians 3:28). Therefore the name of 'Father' will also stand for 'Mother' and 'Son' for 'Daughter' respectively where applicable.

This generation has been branded 'fatherless' and I believe there are thousands of emerging apostles that have gifts within them and they are not being released because we don't have fathers that understand the apostolic calling and the need to release them like we should. This can be argued on the contrary too. The few spiritual fathers who are there can argue that their to-be sons have no sonship qualities in them and that's the reason they have not helped them.

There is a great abuse of fatherhood in the Church today. That's why businesses are collapsing, pastors and the to-be pastors are morally corrupted, marriages are breaking and divorce rate in the church is high. (We have so many immature fathers and so many spiritual orphans in churches today.

Paul was categorical when he addressed this matter to the church of Corinth. The church of Corinth was going through what the today church is going through. He said,

I do not write these things to shame you, but as my beloved children, I warn you. For though you might have ten thousand instructors in Christ, yet you do not have many fathers; for in Christ Jesus I have begotten you through the gospel. Therefore I urge you to imitate me. **1 Corinthians 4:14-16**

To have an instructor (mentor) does not make him your spiritual father. Before you submit to someone for fathering you must know the difference. If you do not know the difference you may be seriously abused.

You derive your DNA from your father. It is your father's seed that determines who you become. The spiritual seed from your spiritual father produces the spiritual you. Your biological father provided basic necessities of life, spent valuable time with you, and shared valuable lessons of life with you as he was taught and experienced. The same applies to a spiritual father.

Some of you have joined yourselves to spiritual fathers whom you share no spiritual DNA with and you are now being treated as a orphans. Each time sons approach their fathers, they are openly received, but bastards are treated with contempt and shame because of where and how they were gotten.

Spiritual Fatherhood is more than Tithes and Offerings

The reason why some are into fatherhood is because of the financial gain derived from such sons. They are only interested in the percentage of the income that comes from their 'sons'. To those fathers, whether the son lives or dies, they are working or not, their businesses are doing well or not, is irrelevant to them. The only attachment they have with them is their money. No money no father.

How can you call someone your father who hardly prays with you but is only interested in your money? How can you call someone your father who never introduces you to the spiritual discipline of his life for you to learn from? How can you call someone your father who never allowed you to know how they failed in their venture in serving Christ or in the business and career world?

Parenting is not only about success; it is about failure too. Spiritual parents are to let their sons/daughters know their challenges which the good Lord through His grace helped them overcome.

True fathers prepare their sons to know what will happen after their departure so that their sons can be aware of it.

They warn their sons, challenge them, pray with them, carry them in their bosoms, and discipline them when necessary.

Fatherhood is more than receiving; it is also about giving - giving of time and money. I am proud of my spiritual father Reverend Chris Musau who gave his time and sometimes money when I was low and needed help. He never allowed me to suffer shame, but treated me as son. Such fathers deserve double honour! And when we are blessed and financially lifted, not to financially bless such fathers is a sin and a curse.

If you have a spiritual father, what made you call him your father? Some of you have gone for fathers because they have great influence and power in ministry. Some have gone for fathers because they are known around the world, or because they are on national TV. Others have gone for fathers to use their connections while you don't mind the wrong doctrine they preach.

Is he your Spiritual Father?

Someone prayed for you to receive Christ; is he your spiritual father? According to me, it's a 'yes' and a 'no' answer. If the one who prayed the repentance prayer did not bring you up in ministry or nurture you spiritually, then no; that person was only used by God to help you receive Christ but not to father you. The truth is: bringing up a child is more tasking than giving birth. More honour is due to the one who spends more time, energy, and resources making you a man from a boy, a woman from a daughter and a minister from a believer. That is truly your father.

A father can be identified by the following roles according to Paul - protection, guidance, instruction, correction, exhortation, encouragement, and inspiration. Has the person you call your father done these things to you? Be careful of the many people who want to reap where they never planted. People who, when you were weak and wretched, hopeless and broken, did nothing to shape you into a better person. But now that you are blessed, anointed, blessed with money, and are an honourable person, they want to call you 'son' and be associated with you at the expense of your real father.

Apolos and Cephas could not have become the spiritual fathers of the Corinthian Church even though they had preached relentlessly to them; Paul had a full responsibility as a father over that church even though he was far away.

Many preachers go to churches, invited as visiting preachers, and start forming sons and daughters in those churches. This is craftiness. Nobody should eat your tithe except your father who takes care of your spiritual needs; not even those who just come preaching and prophesying for one day or a week.

Responsibilities of a Spiritual Father

Check the qualifications below to see the responsibilities of a father and then classify the man or woman you call father or mother. Paul had a fourfold responsibility as a spiritual father to his sons in Corinth. He was responsible to warn them, exhort them, set an example for them, and discipline them.

> *I do not write these things to shame you, but as my beloved children, I warn you. For though you might have ten thousand instructors in Christ, yet you do not have many fathers;*

for in Christ Jesus I have begotten you through the gospel.
Therefore I urge you to imitate me
1 Corinthians 4:14-16

i. A Spiritual Father warns his Sons (see 1 Corinthians 4:14)

Paul was pretty rough with the Corinthians in this chapter. He had resorted to using biting sarcasm to show them their proud and haughty spirit that they might repent. However, his real point in this was not because he viewed them as his enemies and wanted to shame them, but because he viewed them as his children and wanted to warn them. He was not prompted by bitterness to write as he had, but by love. A true father will do the same to his true sons. This is definitely the art of success for you. Your father should warn you if you don't pay your tithes, or if you don't love and forgive others, and will not allow you to be destroyed for lack of knowledge. Our spiritual fathers can see dangers that we may not see. If he warns you of a relationship, don't argue with him for what he can see, you may not see.

Sometimes my spiritual father has warned me of things that endanger me. It takes discipline to obey him. Though the danger he claims is not visible to me, after some time what he had predicted comes to pass. Suppose I had not obeyed? Then I would be a victim of the course.

What fathers can see while asleep, sons can't see while standing. Before I learnt to obey as a son, I fell into many traps that my father had warned me of. Thank God he never gave up on me until I learnt not to doubt his words.

Paul as a father needed to warn the Corinthian Church that their pride and arrogance was only going to hurt them and the body of Christ. If not checked, it would result in schisms in the body of Christ. As a spiritual father or mother you must be willing to make the hard decision at times, and firmly warn your sons of the spiritual dangers they are exposing themselves to. This should be done out of love.

ii. A Spiritual Father exhorts his sons (1 Corinthians 4:16)

Therefore I urge you... the word 'urge' means —to exhort to a course of action, or —to encourage. That which Paul was urging them to do was to follow his example. The Bible teaches us that we should exhort (encourage) one another day after day so that none are hardened by the deceitfulness of sin (see Hebrews 3:13). When we meet together as a church it is for the purpose of exhorting one another. Teaching the Word is essential for a healthy church, but mutual exhortation is no less important.

> *Let us not give up meeting together, as some are in the habit of doing, but let us encourage one another -and all the more as you see the day approaching.* **Hebrews 10:25**

A father exhorts his sons in many ways. He may exhort his son in business, in pursuing education, in working hard, trusting God, repenting of sin, obeying the Word, using their spiritual gifts, serving others, forgiving those that have wronged them, persevering in trials, praying without ceasing, studying the Word, sharing their faith, and giving to the poor

iii. A Spiritual Father sets an example for his sons (1 Corinthians 4:16-17)

Imitate me...This refers to Paul's description of himself and his ministry.

> *We work hard with our own hands. When we are cursed, we bless; when we are persecuted, we endure it; when we are slandered, we answer kindly; up to this moment, we have become the scum of the earth, the refuse of the world.* 1 **Corinthians 4:12-13**

Paul had many things that could be imitated by his sons. His toiling, working with his hands, blessing when he was reviled, enduring when he was persecuted, conciliating when he was slandered, etc. Spiritual fathers should have a life to be imitated by their sons. *For this reason I have sent to you Timothy... he will remind you of my ways which are in Christ* Paul adds to them.

Paul loved his sons so much that he was not content just sending them a letter. He wanted them to have someone who could help them with their issues. He sent them the one person whom he knew was a true son as we will see later. Timothy was sent to remind them of Paul's ways.

A biological father knows that he must set a good example for his children because if his life contradicts his words, his children are far more likely to follow his bad example than his good teaching. Thus, a spiritual father will seek to set an example for his children by being a hard worker, being faithful to his wife, and being humble and respectful toward others among other aspects of life.

iv. A Spiritual Father disciplines his sons (1 Corinthians 4:18-21)

Shall I come to you with a rod or with love and a spirit of gentleness?

All of us who are fathers or mothers know that there are many times when we must go further than just warning, exhorting, or setting a good example. If all these fail, we must discipline our children – we must use the shepherd's rod. We must do whatever is necessary to change their course and help them amend their ways. Sometimes this takes the form of a spanking, putting them on restriction, or denying them certain privileges. Such is an example of a true spiritual father.

> *...for what son is not disciplined by his father? If you are not disciplined (and everyone undergoes discipline) then you are illegitimate children and not true sons.* **Hebrews 12:7b, 8**

When a father takes his knife to shape the character of a son, it's not to harm him. It's to release a greater flow of life. True spiritual fathers go to any length to see their spiritual sons become who God called them to be, risking their own lives even in difficult conditions. A true father will cut away the flesh (circumcise) from his son that would impede the flow of life.

Spiritual fathers love their sons by correcting them when they mess up and not talking behind their backs to others because of their own insecurity, or turn political through the divide and rule system.

For a long time I stayed obedient to my spiritual father. I was very close to him and never gave the devil a chance to expose his weaknesses to me. This was so until someday when I listened to people tell me who and how my father was. Satan wanted to destroy my long-lived relationship with my father. When the negatives about my father were said to me, I started being pessimistic; I relaxed in church leadership and began to see his weaknesses instead of the good father I used to know. Many Sundays I exempted myself, going to preach in other churches and trying to avoid the church I had grown spiritually. I then decided to leave and start my own church. Telling my idea to many who knew my ministry, they supported me. I had started detaching myself from the father who exhorted me in ministry, who had discovered the ministry in me, who had stood by me when I was despised and desperate, who made me what I am, and who had convinced the church that I was worthy to be called a pastor. As I preached in other churches, I was invited to speak in revival meetings in one of the mega churches of Redeemed Gospel Churches in the city.

The mistake we sons make is this - when we start rebelling, we go to the same people our fathers introduced us to and try to justify our acts. This time I landed in the hands of a pastor who knew how to observe protocol and honoured authority. He called my spiritual father and told him that he had invited me to speak in his church. He also asked if he had released me with blessings. My father said he had not and that he should not host me. The host pastor called me and told me about the discussion with my spiritual father. I burned with anger and tried to justify myself. I argued that my father was meddling with my affairs, and that I had a right to preach where I wanted. This pastor and his wife sat me down and spoke to me as to a co-minister of the gospel. Among the things they told me was to bury my immature plans of starting a church against my spiritual father's wish, and to humble and apologise to my father even for the things I thought I was right about. Finally they advised me never to listen to negative reports about my father. I did exactly that; my father lovingly forgave me and received me back. I have since been at peace and totally healed of rebellious ways.

Relationship reflected

During all this time that I was not in good terms with him, I struggled in my business and faced serious battles. As I organised the Kenya Diaspora Investment Conference in UK, opposition arose from a government officer who tried to sabotage what I had worked on for months. I remembered I was trying to oppose my father and contribute to the collapse of a ministry he had built and toiled for many years. When I humbled and repented to my spiritual father, my plans began to work. Wisdom came upon me as it came on Joshua after being laid hands on by his father Moses. The Lord prepared a table before my enemies and gave me a landslide of a victory. I easily got my Visa to the UK which I had been denied before. —Do to others what you would like others do to you, was the message.

Our businesses, jobs, and day-to-day lives reflect our relationships with our spiritual fathers. As weak as your spiritual father is, even if he falls into sin, he is still your father. Honour him, pray for him, and cover him.

Cover your father, don't expose his nakedness.

Noah a man of the soil proceeded to plant a vineyard. When he drank some of its wine, he became drunk and lay uncovered inside his tent. Ham the father of Canaan saw his father's nakedness and told his two brothers outside. But Shem and Japheth took a garment and laid it across their shoulders: then they walked in backward and covered their father's nakedness. Their faces were turned the other way so that they would not see their father's nakedness. When Noah awoke from his wine and found out what his youngest son had done to him, he said, —Cursed be Canaan, the lowest of slaves will he be to his brothers. He also said —...may the Lord extend the territory of Japheth... **Genesis 9:20-27**

Who do you choose to be like - Ham or Japheth? Refuse to see and expose the nakedness of your natural or spiritual father; rather cover him whenever people intend to expose him. Always protect him and make him feel secure that he has a son. Some fathers feel threatened having some sons around since all they see in them are mistakes to speak about. Whether you found your father naked or you know his weakness, refuse to be part of exposing him to others. Keep your hands clean. You would rather cover him as a son.

How to honour Spiritual Fathers

1. Joshua son of Moses

Now, Joshua son of Nun was filled with the spirit of wisdom because Moses had laid his hands on him. So the Israelites listened to him and did what the Lord commanded Moses. **Deuteronomy 34:9**

Joshua needed someone to lay hands on him to receive God's wisdom. Wisdom is a key to success. In whatever you do, you need God's wisdom. You need a spiritual father to lay hands on you and impart power and wisdom in your life.

People listened to Joshua because he had a father. For people to listen to you, or to gain favor before men, you must have a spiritual father whom you have received in your heart. For your spiritual father to impact your life, you have to respect him and obey him. Joshua's influence was caused by the reasons below:

a. Joshua had a good relationship with God first.

And the LORD spake unto Moses face to face, as a man speaketh unto his friend. And he turned again into the camp: but his servant Joshua, the son of Nun, a young man, departed not out of the tabernacle. **Exodus 33:11** (King James Version)

Joshua had a personal relationship with God which made it easy for him to have a good relationship with his Father Moses. He had devotion with God and that's why he had no problem obeying Moses. We can easily honour our spiritual fathers if we honor God. This releases us for success automatically.

The spiritual controls the physical. If our spiritual life is messed up, our physical will automatically be messed up. Fix the spiritual and enjoy the reflection in the physical.

b. Joshua never gave a negative report to Moses.

Joshua son of Nun and Caleb the son of Jephunneh, who were among those had explored the land tore their clothes and said

> to the entire Israelite assembly, —*The land we passed on and explored is exceedingly good if the Lord is pleased with us, he will lead us to that land, a land flowing with honey and milk, and will give it to us. Only do not rebel against God and do not be afraid of the people of the land, because we will swallow them up. Their protection is gone but the Lord is with us. Do not be afraid* **Numbers 14:6-9**

As a son, you need to be positive minded. Joshua was always positive on the reports he gave to Moses. Other people's negative opinions never influenced him. He was always there for Moses and always principled. If you can't give your father a positive report, keep the negative one you have to yourself.

> *To the pure, all things are pure, but to those who are corrupted and do not believe, nothing is pure. In fact, both their minds and consciences are corrupted.* **Titus 1:15**

If you are negative-minded, you receive everything negatively, including good sermons from your pastor or even simple corrections. We cannot honour our fathers when we see them negatively. Don't allow anything to go through your ears regarding your father. Anything that creates negative images about him, lock it out. Be like Japheth and not like Ham the sons of Noah. Ask God to give you understanding to see good things and be positive-minded so that you can give your pastor good reports.

c. Joshua obeyed Moses ungrudgingly

As a son, you should have the capacity to respond quickly to your spiritual father's instructions. Numbers 14:6-9 clearly shows that Joshua knew the heart of Moses. He also responded quickly to Moses' instructions on all occasions. This led to the success and influence of Joshua as a leader after Moses. This 'servant of Moses', as the scripture calls him, rose above failure through the art of honouring his spiritual father. Joshua never questioned Moses' instructions, but obeyed them to the letter. Incase you have a different idea from your pastor's, obey him first as long as it is not leading you to sin or ungodliness then humbly come later and explain your opinion. Many times sons engage their fathers in heated arguments which lead to more ungodliness. Always be an example to others in commitment and obedience to your father.

A good son pays his tithes faithfully. This is the first sign of love, commitment, and obedience not only to God, but also to your father. Knowing that your pastors as Levites depend on tithes, you should then be faithful in tithing always. Your faithfulness is seen clearly through your tithe. You can't love your pastor and withhold your tithe. You are starving your pastor. Your commitment is also seen through attendance to church and your service to the ministry. If you are committed to the church, you will arrive earlier than your pastor and leave after your pastor has left. This is mostly so for those who serve in the church as leaders. The blessings translate to your life. Your business, job, education, and everything else can be affected positively or negatively by how you commit yourself in God's work.

d. Joshua never opposed Moses

When Miriam and Aaron opposed Moses in Numbers 12, Joshua never indulged himself in their rebellion. Though Miriam and Aaron felt justified to complain about the wife of Moses who was a Cushite and not an Israelite (God had warned them not to intermarry with other tribes), Joshua's decision not to raise a finger against Moses was a better choice.

Sometimes you have justified reasons to oppose your father but my advice is even then don't try. God's servants have been lifted to a level where we should leave them to God to judge them and never their sons or daughters in ministry. It's only that these days, church members, politicians, and the society don't honour spiritual leaders. During the times of Samuel, Jeremiah, Isaiah, and the other prophets, servants of God were known as 'seers'. They were honoured even by the kings for they represented God Almighty. Even when a servant of God was wrong, God sent a higher spiritual authority to warn them. See the story of David in 2 Samuel 12.

This is why Governments are failing, businesses are stagnating and running bankrupt, and people are being retrenched right, left, and center. Keep reading and see the way back to the true art of success.

2. Shammah and the three sons of David

Know the desire of your father and fight to fulfill it. Shammah, a son of David in the ministry, understood the desire of his father. Though David had only a wish, a very close son like Shammah could hear the wish; he risked and fought to fulfill it.

And David longed for water and said, —Oh that someone would get me a drink of water from the well of Bethlehem! So the three mighty men broke through the philistine lines, drew water from the well near the gate of Bethlehem and carried it back to David. But he refused to drink it; instead he poured it out before the Lord. —Far be it from me, O Lord to do this! he said. —Is it not the blood of men who went at the risk of their lives? And David would not drink it. **2 Samuel 23:15-17**

Many fathers today have desires that no one is willing to fulfill or even to listen to. A true son will sacrifice anything to save his father. There may be many instructors but you have only one father. There are many preachers and pastors, but you have only one father. Take care of him, know his heart desires, and crave to fulfill them.

These sons of David gave his kingship a strong support to extend it over the whole land of Israel as the Lord promised (see 1 Chronicles 11:10-19). They became mighty in Israel because of honouring their father David (see 1 Chronicles 11:10).

Joab stood by his father David. David had other sons too. They were faced by a challenge of their own father falling into sin. When David sinned with Bathsheba, God struck the child born out of the act dead. This was a sin clear to everybody, but the sons of David, the people he had trained in war and ministry, never departed from him. They never turned their back against him. They were with David even when he was fasting and praying.

The elders of his household stood beside him to get him up from the ground but he refused and he would not eat any food with them. **2 Samuel 12:17**

> David noticed that his servants were whispering among themselves...
> (That is to mean they were always close to him)
> **2 Samuel 12:19**

> Meanwhile Joab fought against Rabbah of the Amorites and captured the royal citadel. Joab then sent messengers to David saying, —I have fought against Rabbah and taken its water supply...
> **2 Samuel 12:26-27**

These sons of David were with him and for him even after knowing what he had done. They encouraged him and watched over him. As some took care of him, others like Joab were taking care of the work of their father David. Joab didn't allow the enemies to break in just because their father has been found in a mess.

Sons should encourage, protect, and stand by their fathers in good or bad times. A father will recover faster when he knows there are sons standing by him. When we provide security for our fathers they get time to pray and put things right with God. If Joab could have relaxed, David would have gotten worried about the Amalekites and fail to get time with God. When sons take their positions, fathers get time to hear from the Lord.

Don't take advantage of your father's shortcomings to make a 'name' for yourself or to climb to his position. God deals with His servants in His own way so don't make judgments by what you see or hear. In 2 Samuel 15 this is how Absalom conspired to take over his fathers throne. Little did he know that his father David had been forgiven by God and that God was still with him. Finally Absalom died a miserable death because of opposing his father and planning to overthrow him.

> *Now Absalom happened to meet David's men, He was riding his mule, and as the mule went under the thick branches of a large oak, Absalom's head got caught in the tree. He was left hanging in the midair, while the mule he was riding kept on going......Joab said, "I'm not going to wait like this for you." So he took three javelins in his hand and plunged them into Absalom's heart while Absalom was still alive in the oak tree. And ten of Joab's armor-bearers surrounded Absalom, struck him and killed him.* **2 Samuel 18:9, 14-15**

3. Paul's Spiritual Sons

Paul had many spiritual sons, some of whom he has highlighted in his epistles as either good or bad examples. Good examples of Paul's sons include:

a. Epaphras

> *Epaphras, who is one of you and a servant of Christ Jesus, sends greetings. He is always wrestling in prayer for you, that you may stand firm in all the will of God, mature and fully assured.* **Colossians 4:12**

Paul acknowledges his son Epaphras because of the role he played in his life. He contributed a lot towards the growth of the church, fought and wrestled for the church, and prayed for the church.

Wrestling is fighting; it is important as son to fight for the Church, stand in the gap, and stop the devil from taking over the Church. A true son does exactly that on behalf of his father. He/she stands for the Church not against the Church. He helps his father in growing the ministry by praying for him and the Church.

Epaphras was with his father Paul when he wrote the epistle to the Colossians. This means that he accompanied Paul and prayed together with him when necessary. Disloyal and rebellious sons don't love prayer especially for the church and their pastor (father). People don't like the ministry of prayer because nobody knows when you are praying. They love positions that will make the pastor see that they are active. On the contrary, a father loves it when he knows there is a son praying for him and with him for the church.

Paul knew that Epaphras was praying, because he was loyal and close to his father. Even when you are praying for the church, let your pastor know. Ask him for his burning needs to pray for. You must be secretive; intercessors don't talk carelessly with anybody. This is a very sensitive ministry and a rewarding one too. Though you are busy in your job, find time to stand with your spiritual father in prayer. Let him/her know you are doing it. It shall reciprocate in the success of your business, ministry, job, or education.

As a son never associate with negative-minded people in the church. Epaphras was faithful and wrestled for the church instead of talking about it or tearing it down. Avoid political people in the church. People who talk ill about the pastor are to be avoided, for they are being used by the devil to tear the church down. Always remember he is your father. If there is any problem in the church or with him, pray and wrestle like Epaphras.

b. Timothy

You, however, know all my teaching my way of life, my purpose, faith, patience, love, endurance, persecutions, sufferings-what kinds of things happened to me in Antioch, Iconium, and Lystra, the persecutions I endured. Yet the Lord rescued me from all of them. **2 Timothy 3:10-11**

The relationship between Paul and Timothy his son was outstanding and offers a unique example of spiritual sonship. Like Timothy who knew the teachings, purpose, faith, patience, love, endurance, persecutions, and sufferings of his father Paul, we too ought to know the same of our fathers. A true son knows his father, and this is the beginning of honour.

i. Timothy knew the teachings of his father Paul

As a son you need to know the teachings of your father. When you know your father's teachings, you will not say he lacks revelation or creativity or anointing. That is his way of teaching. For instance, some pastors teach slowly while others can be loud and powerful. Some are revivalists, others are miracle workers, others encouragers, etc. To understand your father's teaching is of paramount importance so that you can learn to receive him as he is.

Many people criticise their pastor for not being anointed like pastor so-and-so, or not having a gift of working miracles like another pastor. You must understand your pastor's teachings and know the gifts he operates in. He can't be like another pastor. You need to understand that God calls His servants differently. If your biological father was a taxi driver, that's your father and you can never change him to a senator or a pilot; you have to love him as he is. So is it with spiritual fathers.

And he gave some, apostles; and some, prophets; and some, evangelists; and some, pastors and teachers; for the perfecting of the saints, for the work of the ministry, for the edifying of the body of Christ
Ephesians 4:12

Now to each one, the manifestation of the spirit is given to the common good. To one there is given through the spirit the message of wisdom, to another the message of knowledge by means of the spirit, to another faith by the same spirit, to another gift of healing by that one spirit, to another miraculous powers, to another prophesy, to another distinguishing between spirits......all these are the works of one and the same spirit, and he gives them to each one, as he determines.
1 Corinthians 12:7-11

God gives you a father with divine reasons and chooses which gifts to operate in him. A son may rise up to be a better preacher than his father. Even then honor him. Juanita Bynum while preaching in her father's conference confessed, —I was proud when I thought I was anointed, until the Lord told me I operated under the grace of my father Bishop Jakes. She added, —People should stop ranking servants of God by the way they minister, there are spiritual authorities to honour, and I can never be equal to my father.

Honour your father because he can speak success to you when you are cursed to failure. He can plead to the Lord on your behalf but he can also reject you before the Lord.

Due to disloyalty, people don't follow their pastor's doctrine. If your pastor operates under one or more of the above gifts, you need to know it and stop comparing him to others.

Timothy knew his father's teachings because he always followed him and listened to him. Even when he was not near him, he enquired of what was happening to him. He had a friendly relationship with his father and so should we.

ii. Timothy knew the purpose of Paul

As a son you should know the purpose of your spiritual father. Know your pastor's dream and be able to interpret it. One man dreams at a time while others interpret the dream. Like Joshua, to interpret is to be able to run with the dream even after your father is gone, and fulfill what he intended.

Remember if you have your own dream it should be in line with that of your father and must grow under the dream of your father until he sees it fit to release you. Even after he has released you to follow your dream, he still has authority over you to correct you, rebuke you, and shape you.

If sons are left to do things on their own before they are mature they often bring shame to the Church family. The father should issue directives including limits which sons should observe. The sons of prophets whom Elisha was a father to had to go with him to Jordan. Even when the idea benefits the church, fathers should be consulted first to give advice and directives. When things go wrong they can then intervene. But if you ignore them and meet challenges, fathers should not be used as a last option.

And the sons of the prophets said unto Elisha, —Behold now, the place where we dwell with thee is too strait for us. Let us go, we pray thee, unto Jordan, and take thence every man a beam, and let us make us a place there, where we may dwell. And he answered, —Go ye. And one said, —Be content, I pray thee, and go with thy servants. And he answered (Elisha replied), —I will go. But as one was felling a beam, the axe head fell into the water: and he cried, and said, —Alas, master! For it was borrowed. And the man of God said —Where fell it? And he showed him the place. And he cut down a stick, and cast it in thither; and the iron did swim. Therefore said he, —Take it up to thee. And he put out his hand, and took it. **2 Kings 6:1-7** (King James Version)

iii. Timothy knew the patience of Paul

Fathers should be patient with the weak sons. Give them time to change and become better. Sons should as well learn from the fathers regarding being patient with the weak. Timothy knew about suffering and the love of his father Paul. Though Timothy was not with Paul in Antioch, he was so close to him that he knew what was happening to him.

It is important to call or visit your father as regularly as possible and know how he is doing. Encourage him and remind him that, —Dad I'm praying for you, we are together. Pastors go through a lot of suffering and loneliness and when you call him and encourage him it is refreshing. Don't call your spiritual father only when you have a problem or you need prayers. Call him even for a word of encouragement. It is not enough to see your pastor only on Sunday. Timothy could never have known how Paul was doing if he only met him once a week or never inquired about him. Timothy was a close follower of his 'pastor' 'father' Paul.

Observe your pastor's character, speech, dressing, and doctrine, and follow it. Paul always told Timothy 'you know' because they shared one mind.

> *You know that every one in the province of Asia has deserted me including Phygelus and Hermogenes.* **2 Timothy 1:15**

c. Onesiphorus

> *May the Lord show mercy to the household of Onesiphorus, because he often refreshed me and was not ashamed of my chains. On the contrary when he was in Rome, he searched hard for me until he found me. May the Lord grant that he will find mercy from the Lord in that day. You know very well in how many ways he helped me in Ephesus.*
> **2 Timothy 1:16-18**

What testimony can your father give about you? What kind of prayer can he make for you before God? Paul prayed to God to grant Onesiphorus mercy on the Day of Judgment. These are called untouchables. Some sons are untouchables of their fathers because of what they do to them. Someone said, —There are people in my church who, if Satan attacks them, I would rather face the devil on their behalf than allow him to touch them. In other words he had better suffer than for them to suffer. These are the Onesiphorus kind. At the same time there are others who even when they are in trouble, he will not be moved much to act. The difference is caused by what the sons do to their father.

i. Onesiphorus always refreshed his spiritual father Paul.

The word 'refresh' means 'to restore with fresh supply, make cool again, as to someone'. This means that Paul was in distress when Onesiphorus refreshed him. When we go to see our fathers, we should not go empty-handed. It refreshes your father when you bless him with a gift. This can be a material gift or money. Buy him/her a suit, do shopping for his house, or go with a token and tell him —Daddy/Mommy, I love you. In return, the words he will speak upon your life will be powerful and will cause your success.

Saul, though he had not established the sonship relationship with Samuel, knew fathers as prophets are not seen emptyhanded.

> *Then said Saul to his servant, —But, behold, if we go, what shall we bring the man? For the bread is spent in our vessels, and there is not a present to bring to the man of God; what have we? And the servant answered Saul again, and said, —Behold, I have here at hand the fourth part of a shekel of silver; that will I give to the man of God, to tell us our way.* **1 Samuel 9:7-8**

ii. He was not ashamed about the chains of his father Paul

Our fathers are made from clay like anybody else, and they can have shortcomings. Your father is happy when you are not ashamed of his/her shortcomings, just like Onesiphorus. Sons must be careful how they react when their fathers are faced by shortcomings, especially when they are accused of sin or any other external force fighting the ministry. By so saying I am not justifying sin. Come to think of it, when sons are caught in a mess, they run to their fathers for prayers and they expect their father to cover their reputation. To whom shall the father run when faced by the same scenario? We may say they will run to their fathers, but sons have the a key role to play. Fight and protect your father at all costs. Be a Japheth, a son of Noah, and not a Ham.

iii. Onesiphorus searched for his father Paul in Rome

Be a son who can search for your father. Encourage him, keep him company. Carry his briefcase like Elisha. It is this closeness that makes sons get the mantle when the father gets ready to pass it on. Do not be like Gehazi who only looked at what his father had, until he lost his inheritance because of deceiving Naaman behind his father Elisha's back.

Fathers love to share with their sons. This shows them that you love them too. Love is a two-way traffic; as your father loves you, love him back. Let this love be genuine and without hypocrisy as the Bible says. You can play hypocrisy with your pastor but you can't do it with God. He shall shame you by exposing your ill motives.

Other good sons of Paul are Stephanas, Fortunatus, and Achaicus.

> *I am glad of the coming of Stephanas and Fortunatus and Achaicus: for that which was lacking on your part they have supplied.*
> **1 Corinthians 16:17**

As there are good examples of sons that can be emulated in the Bible, there are others who were bad news to their fathers. We have seen Absalom and Gehazi briefly.

Bad examples of Paul's sons include:

a. Demas

> *Do your best to come to me quickly, for Demas, because he loved this world, has deserted me and has gone to Thesalonica. Crescens has gone Galatia, and Titus to Dalmatia. Only Luke is with me. Get Mark and him with you because he is helpful to me in my ministry*
> **2 Timothy 4:9**

Paul cried to Timothy one of his sons and told him of what Demas, another son of his, did to him. It is too unfortunate for us to make our spiritual fathers have pain in their hearts. Some problems we have in our businesses, jobs, or ministries are because we choose our way and disobey our spiritual fathers. My spiritual father told me never to rebel because I would make him sick. This is because when our true fathers choose to love us, they open their hearts and secrets to us. It hurts and pains when we rebel and choose our own ways like Demas. Demas deserted his father Paul when Paul needed him most. Some you sons desert your fathers when they need you most. There are times your father is in need and he expects you to stand by him, and if you don't, then you are deserting him like Demas. We should be consistent in the support of our fathers, not sending our support in January and remembering to do so again in August. Some sons desert their fathers when they are in need, but they return when they are in trouble to ask for blessings and cover. Walk in integrity with your father.

A father needs a son he can trust with information and his private life. Do not strip naked your father when he tells his secrets. Avoid the 'Ham syndrome' and always remember to imitate Japheth; the sons of Noah.

b. Alexander

Alexander the metal worker did me a great deal of harm, the Lord will repay him for what he has done. You too should on your guard for him, because he strongly opposed our message. **2 Timothy 4:14**

The name Alexander means 'a defender of men', but Alexander didn't do things according to his name. Like many sons today, he opposed the message of his father Paul. You will not be surprised today when sons compare themselves with their fathers. The question of who can preach better, who is more anointed, who has the best car, who has what and doesn't have what should never be heard between a son and father, spiritual or not spiritual.

—Abner, whose son is that young man?.... the King said, —
Find out whose son this young man is. **1 Samuel 17:55, 56**

Fathers bring up sons to become better than them; they mentor them to their destiny. It is my dream that where I reached in education, business, and ministry, my son may continue further and be better than me. It will be wrong for my son to start comparing himself to me or engaging himself in a competition with me. Fathers give up their names for their sons so that their sons can carry on the name. That's why Saul asked —Whose son is that young man? when David killed Goliath.

As Saul watched David going out to meet the philistine, he
said to Abner, commander of the army, —Abner, whose son is
that young man?.... the King said, —Find out whose son this
young man is.
1 Samuel 17:55, 56

The achievements of a son were and should still be credited to his father. Today sons want to take all the glory. These are the Alexander-kind. This hurt Paul so much as a father. Fathers mostly find us when we hardly know anything. They train us until we become strong and exposed like Alexander. When we rebel against our fathers it breaks their heart. Paul leaves Alexander to God to repay him for what he did to him. This is the last word you would want to hear from your spiritual father. Spiritual fathers have been favored by God to plead on your behalf as well as to deny you and you will be denied in heaven.

When God wanted to wipe out the tribe of Israel for rebelling against Him, Moses pleaded with God on their behalf and God spared them. In Numbers 16, when Korah, Dathan, and Abiram and their supporters rebelled against Moses, they were swallowed up by the earth. When God stands in defense for His servants, things turn ugly.

Paul warned Timothy and other sons to stay away from Alexander because of his conduct. This is what should be done to sons who oppose their father's doctrine. Fathers, do not allow rebellion to spread from sons like Alexander.

Holding on to faith and a good conscience some have rejected these and so have shipwrecked their faith. Among them are Hymenaeus and Alexander whom I have handed over to Satan to be taught not to blaspheme. **1 Timothy 1:19**

Sons, stay clean and don't walk in rebellious groups. While Paul depended on Alexander and Hymenaeus to support him in ministry, they instead turned against him. He was hurt when he saw them perishing after being with them for a while. If you have a true spiritual father, then be sure he wishes you good. If you oppose the work of God, God will also oppose you. Your father needs you. If you love your spiritual father, you will support his vision and help in interpreting his dream.

If your senior pastor doesn't treat you like a son just as Paul was to his sons, then that's not a father. Remember Paul's words - you may have many instructors but you only have one father. You had better leave peacefully without influencing others and God shall lead you to your father. The truth is, true spiritual fathers are few. We have more of rent-a-father lifestyle today than true fatherhood.

Ask the person you call your spiritual father, —Who is your spiritual father? Many want to be fathers while they have never been fathered. Some rebelled from their fathers; others are their own fathers. My advise to any sons reading this book is to ask the person you call your father, —Who is your father daddy? If he can't answer that question, then run away from a curse because your biggest inheritance is a big curse of rebellion.

If you are looking for a father here are some wisdom nuggets:

- *Prayerfully approach the matter with eternity in mind*

For you to call anyone your spiritual father without prayerfully considering the effect is like asking for someone to come in and rob you. It is God who determined who our natural father will be. We did not have a choice in the matter. So also it is divinely relevant for you not to rush to choose by the dictation of your flesh whom your spiritual father should be until you pray through. The person you call your father can make you or destroy you. You must approach the subject with heaven in mind. If you have a father who is not heavenly-minded, there is the tendency that you might miss it also. Remember, like father like son! You become after your father unless you choose to be different. Follow Paul's example of a Father's responsibility to know where you are to locate your spiritual Father.

- *Know who you are (see 1 Peter 2:4-5)*

If you do not know your worth, you will become a victim of abuse from anyone. Always remember that it took God, your Heavenly Father, the death and blood of His Son, our Lord and Savior, to redeem you and I. You are valuable and significant to Him and it should be so with any spiritual father. Never sell yourself cheap. You are a blood-bought saint of God, chosen, elected, and adopted into the family of the beloved. If your spiritual father does not accept you and treat you as a son, kindly relocate prayerfully and without strife. Remember your success is tied in to your relationship with your spiritual father. Therefore don't make yourself a failure by failing to observe this precious art of success.

- *Reconcile with your Spiritual Father*

And he (Jesus) said, —A certain man had two sons: And the younger of them said to his father, _Father, give me the portion of goods that falleth to me.' And he divided unto them his living. And not many days after the younger son gathered all together, and took his journey into a far country, and there wasted his substance with riotous living. And when he had spent all, there arose a mighty famine in that land; and he began to be in want. And he went and joined himself to a citizen of that country; and he sent him into his fields to feed swine. And he would fain have filled his belly with the husks that the swine did eat: and no man gave unto him. And when he came to himself, he said, _How many hired servants of my father's have bread enough and to spare, and I perish with hunger! I will arise and go to my father, and will say unto him, _Father; I have sinned against heaven, and before thee, and am no more worthy to be called thy son: make me as one of thy hired servants.' And he arose, and came to his father. But when he was yet a great way off, his father saw him, and had compassion, and ran, and fell on his neck, and kissed him. And the son said unto him, _Father, I have sinned against heaven, and in thy sight, and am no more worthy to be called thy son.' But the father said to his servants, _Bring forth the best robe, and put it on him; and put a ring on his hand, and shoes on his feet: And bring hither the fatted calf, and kill it; and let us eat, and be merry: For this my son was dead, and is alive again; he was lost, and is found.' And they began to be merry. **Luke 15:11-24** (King James Version)

The story of the prodigal son is an example of an immature ambitious son. He thought he was wise and so he followed his desires. Maybe you felt like you were ready to go it on your own, maybe your spiritual father warned you against some action, and you still did it against his/her wish. This is the day to go back to him and make it up with him/her. It is never too late to apologize because that is what is holding your success.

Regardless of who was right or who had hurt who, swallow your pride and humble yourself before your father. You may not go back to his ministry but let him pronounce blessings to you. When you go to reconcile with a spiritual authority, you don't go empty-handed. And may the Lord prosper you in whatever you do.

Conclusion

You are the architect of your own success. Don't give excuses for not living successfully. People have succeeded without much of the things you are still waiting for to start your journey to success. Look for at least one reason to succeed and go for it.

- THE END -

Bibliography

1. Maxwell, John C. *Developing the Leader Within You.* n.p Nashville, TN. 1993. Print.
2. Wattles, Wallace D. *The Science of Getting Rich.* n.p. Ohio. 1910. Print.
3. Kiyosaki, Robert T., Lechter, Sharon L. *Rich Dad, Poor Dad.* Techpress. Kittrell, NC. 2003. Print.
4. Covey, Stephen R. *The Seven Habits of Highly Effective People.* Simon & Schuster. New York, NY. 1989. Print.
5. Warren, Rick. *The Purpose Driven Life.* n.p. Grand Rapids, MI. 2002. Print.
6. Mason, John. *You're Born an Original -Don't die a copy.* n.p. Grand Rapids, MI. 1993. Print.
7. Mason, John. *You Can Do It, Even If Others Say You Can't.* n.p. Grand Rapids, MI. 2003. Print.
8. Armstrong, Tracey. *Becoming a Pioneer of Success.* n.p. Seattle, WA. 2005. Print.
9. Ziglar, Zig. *See You at the Top.* Magna Publishing Co. Ltd. Dallas, TX. 2000. Print.

Other Readings

Green, R., Elfers J. *The 48 Laws of Power.* n.p. New York. 2010. Print.

Haanel, Charles F. *The Master Key System.* Psychology Publishing. St. Louis, MO. 1912. Print.

Mwangi, J.N., Omollo, M.O. *How to Start & Manage Your Own Business.* n.p. Nairobi. 2007. Print.

Person, Marnie L. *Nothing is Impossible For Those Who Believe.*.n.p. 2004. Print.

Printed in the United States
By Bookmasters